BELIEVE the WOMEN

A Journey of Liberation with Alliance of Baptists' Women

LEAH GRUNDSET DAVIS

© 2019

Published in the United States by Nurturing Faith Inc., Macon GA,
www.nurturingfaith.net.

Library of Congress Cataloging-in-Publication Data is available.

ISBN 978-1-63528-063-0

All scripture quotations are from New Revised Standard Version Bible, copyright © 1989 National Council of the Churches of Christ in the United States of America. Used by permission. All rights reserved worldwide.

All rights reserved. Printed in the United States of America

*For Lydia Ellen and Sadie Pearl,
may you always keep singing the song of justice-love and
live into exactly whom you are created to be.*

Contents

Acknowledgments 1
Foreword 3
Introduction and How to Use This Study 7
Context & History of the Alliance of Baptists 11
Week One: Hope 17
Week Two: Peace 27
Week Three: Joy 49
Week Four: Love 67
Week Five: Promise 93
Leader's Guide/Lesson Plan ....
Sermon Series and Worship Planning 105
Sermon Series and Worship Services
    for the Seasons of Advent and Christmas 114
For More Information 129

Acknowledgments

To bring these stories into fruition has been holy and sacred for me. As I met with each of these preachers, I heard their passion and their commitment to living out the liberating faith of Jesus. Over and over again I have returned to their words for encouragement, for hope, and for the promises of God as Mary understood them. I believe Mary in her song at the beginning of Luke, and Mary Magdalene in her preaching at the end of Luke that Jesus had risen. I believe these women as they proclaim who God is, who they are, and the place where those two meet. To Rev. Nancy Hastings Sehested, Rev. Dr. Isabel Docampo, Rev. April Baker, Rev. Kyndra Frazier, Rev. Maria Swearingen, and Rev. Molly Brummett Wudel, thank you for trusting me with your stories of faith, identity, and proclamation.

I am grateful to so many people who have walked this far with me on this journey already. To my Alliance of Baptists friends and colleagues—Carole Collins, Rev. Paula Clayton Dempsey, Cathy McGaughey, Rev. Dr. Ken Meyers, Kristy Pullen, Rev. Toya Richards, and Rev. Jason Smith—thank you for your support and dreamings.

To all the early pioneers within the Alliance of Baptists and beyond who kept us moving toward justice, who opened up space for women to preach and pastor and live our callings, thank you. For the readers of this work—Rev. Dr. Kristin Adkins Whitesides, Andrew Gardner, Rev. Dr. Mahan Siler, and Meredith Story Williams—thank you for your time and your edits. To my adviser at Candler School of Theology at Emory University, Dr. Susan Hylen, you learned all about these wild, scrappy Baptists, and your scholarship and witness made this study all the more powerful. My Doctor of Ministry colleagues offered insight, critique, and many laughs along the way—thank you!

To the women who have modeled what it means to be Baptist and preach, especially Rev. Dr. Amy Butler, who wrote the foreword to this book, and Rev. Julie Pennington-Russell, who pastored me as a young seminary student when I thought I might want to be a pastor myself but didn't have any female examples, I am who I am because of your mentoring and friendship. To Dr. Ruth Ann Foster, Dr. Lai Ling Ngan, Dr. Rosalie Beck, and Dr. Sharyn Dowd, who were my professors and life teachers at Baylor University and Truett Seminary, you opened up the Bible to me in new, critical ways that helped me embrace my own calling. And to two Alliance of Baptists congregational partners, which I love dearly and where I've had the privilege to be a pastor—Calvary Baptist Church, Washington, D.C., and Ravensworth Baptist Church, Annandale, Virginia—this world is closer to God's dreams because of you and your witness.

And last, but certainly not least, to my husband, John, and our daughters, Lydia Ellen and Sadie Pearl, you all sent me away for hours and weeks for school and to create this book. Lydia Ellen and Sadie Pearl, you inspire me, and we keep singing Mary's song with hope for all you will proclaim in your lives. There are so many more friends, family, and colleagues who have encouraged me, and for all of you, I give thanks.

Let's keep singing of God's justice-love together.

Bristow, Virginia
October 2018

Foreword

The future is female, as they say.

Apparently, so is the past.

History shows us that as movements are born, they very often involve the voices and leadership of women who work hard to establish new energy and efforts to make our shared human existence more kind and equitable. As movements turn into institutions, however, the voices and leadership of women are increasingly suppressed. It is profound, then, to remember that with the Magnificat, Mary's song, it is the voice of a woman that issues a mandate challenging the powers that oppress, divide, and harm; her words are the very foundation of the work and witness of Jesus Christ in the world.

As we know, hers was a small voice in a loud world with a tendency not to listen. It's a good thing that the voices of women are often revolutionary. Over and over in our collective story, women have called for change and ushered us toward a society that welcomes and nurtures the whole.

Because even before a baby was born, there was a song. Summoned from the deep, fear-filled breaths of a young woman totally marginalized and without any power at all, this song is a faith-filled declaration that paints a picture of her world turned on its head—where everybody had enough to flourish in the task of human living. And perhaps the most miraculous thing of all is that Mary's song is sung—and heard—by Elizabeth, her words landing right and true, offering hope and agency for them both in a time when there was none. In hearing Mary through Elizabeth's ears, we suddenly know that Mary's song is as corporate as it is individual—a new way of seeing the world being born in one person while God is busy birthing a new world for everyone. It's the lives, words, and witness of women changing the world.

It's miraculous.

This book is a collection of theological work, sermons, and personal stories that remind us that we ignore the prophetic voices of women at our own peril, for they have kept—and they will keep—raising their voices and calling us to fix broken systems. It's particularly notable that we're offered this powerful invitation to engage Mary's song through the voices of Baptist women ministers—those who have persisted in their determination to follow God's call in the face of institutions that would silence them.

In words inviting us to a new way of living, we understand again why we are foolish to ignore more than half the witness of humanity—the women—choosing instead to marginalize, contain, diminish, and demean their witness. Women will not keep silent, and we must listen because we need women's voices to do the work of God in the world.

What will it take for us to believe the women?

I am a pastor myself. I grew up in a conservative, evangelical home, an upbringing I credit with so many foundational aspects of my faith. But I never saw a woman exercising ordained leadership in the church. It is profoundly true that you cannot be what you cannot see, so when the persistent call of God began to pull at me, I looked to see whom I could find who was living what I felt called to do. When I chose to become a Baptist, I did it because I was so enamored with the idea that God's spirit will show up wherever she wants, creating new life inside and outside of institutions that have built walls and excluded certain people and tried to harness her work of redemption in the world.

Still, over and over I was told I could not be a pastor—and those voices still issue their critique on a regular basis. But the witness of the women whose voices I heard spoke louder to me; they knew my experience of feeling so convicted of your vocation that you cannot set it aside. Gifted with the friendships and examples of pioneering Baptist women, some of whose voices you will hear in this book, I was gradually able to begin imagining and risking a life of ordained ministry.

Rev. Dr. Leah Grundset Davis, former pastoral intern, colleague of mine, and now accomplished practitioner herself, invites us into this critical conversation about Baptist identity, the voices and witness of women, and the task God has set before us today. One baton after another, handed woman to woman, the same message of inclusion, justice, and peace—what a gift to the world.

In these moments when being a Baptist—and, indeed, being a Christian—is so grievously misrepresented in our culture, all of these women echo the song of Mary, the original resister. It's their voices, and it's Mary's voice speaking to us, calling clearly from the distance of decades and even thousands of years to listen—and to believe her. She's a prophet speaking truth to power, as any of us who claim to follow Jesus should be. And all of their voices give us courage to find our own voice, to take a deep breath, and to tell the truth about injustice in the face of God's dreams for our world.

With this rich witness surrounding and leading us, why wouldn't we believe the women? Why wouldn't we be the women speaking loud and clear and without apology?

So raise your own voice.

And listen.

Listen to these voices. And listen to Mary's song.

And believe them.

Rev. Dr. Amy K. Butler
Senior Minister
Riverside Church, New York City
October 2018

Introduction and How to Use this Study

Our study engages the Magnificat, Mary's song in Luke 1, as an inspirational song for six Alliance of Baptists women preachers. All of these women relate the Magnificat to elements of their identity—as followers of Jesus and as Baptists.

Their experiences of Mary's song highlight themes of Baptist identity, including embodiment in preaching, power and agency in the act of proclamation, and the principle of freedom. For many women in Baptist life, their bodies have been seen as problematic, especially those women who wanted to be pastors.[1]

However, when preaching Mary's Magnificat, a song that Mary sang when her body was seen as problematic by the larger religious world, these Baptist women grasped their full embodiment with power as sermons flowed from their lips and their hearts. They believed God had looked with favor on them, as they are created by God.

Agency and freedom are also strong themes that resonate throughout the conversations about identity. The Alliance of Baptists covenant, an influential document for each of the women, came about in a time when a small group of Baptists had to sing about what they believed in the midst of a swirling, powerful Baptist entity—the Southern Baptist Convention (SBC). When Baptist women speak of the Magnificat, they do so in conversation with their Baptist identity.

As women preach and study this text, in general, they tell the story of Mary as a woman and her own agency and power.

In Luke, Mary sings,

> My soul magnifies the Lord, and my spirit rejoices in God my Savior, for he has looked with favor on the lowliness of his servant. Surely, from now on all generations will call me blessed; for the Mighty One has done great things for me, and holy is his name. His mercy is for those who

> fear him from generation to generation. He has shown strength with his arm; he has scattered the proud in the thoughts of their hearts. He has brought down the powerful from their thrones, and lifted up the lowly; he has filled the hungry with good things, and sent the rich away empty. He has helped his servant Israel, in remembrance of his mercy, according to the promise he made to our ancestors, to Abraham and to his descendants forever. (Luke 1:46–55)

Considering that Mary's trip to visit her cousin Elizabeth and her song of God's faithfulness passed down from one generation to another, we'll read the stories of six women within the Alliance of Baptists who represent a shared commitment to the organization from its birth to the most recent celebrations of life.

Baptist women in ministry have faced an uphill climb for as long as Baptist women have been in ministry. However, since the birth of the Alliance of Baptists in 1987, women in ministry have been affirmed and their voices celebrated. As the organization has grown, so has the presence of women in pulpits and pastorates across the United States. The work of liberation and songs of resistance have always been a part of the Alliance's story and an integral part of the Alliance's covenant.

These generational perspectives sing of God's faithfulness from the pregnancy, birth, and life of this group of Baptists and to individuals. Through conversations with these women, common threads emerged that pointed toward themes of identification of calling, participation in justice issues, and personal connection with the Magnificat as a song of liberation for women.

This study shares six voices that have been previously neglected in our Baptist world by providing a specific focus on Alliance of Baptists' women. It brings into conversation race, sexuality, gender, and identity, which are pressing concerns for each of our lives and the life and health of the church.

When the Alliance of Baptists was formed, the covenant became the guiding document, which highlighted the organization's core distinctives and freedoms. The covenant guides the organization along the way as a type of living, breathing guide, and so it served as a touchpoint in discussions with the six women as a way to come back to Baptist principles. You'll read good, thoughtful critiques and words of gratitude for a document that guides and yet continues to evolve.

Percentagewise, there are more Alliance of Baptists' congregational partners pastored by women than any other Baptist denomination. The Alliance also endorses more women to chaplaincy and pastoral counselor ministry than any other Baptist denomination.[2]

Nearly thirty-one percent of Alliance of Baptists' congregational partners are pastored by women, compared to the Cooperative Baptist Fellowship at five percent, Baptist General Association of Virginia at two percent, and the Baptist General Convention of Texas not even at one-half of one percent. Women have found a home in the Alliance of Baptists and found empowerment from Mary's song.

Together, we'll explore the history of the Alliance, the stories of individual women, and the implications of their stories on the connection between Baptist identity, the Magnificat, and all of our stories.

The six preachers selected to participate in this study range from founders of the Alliance of Baptists to those born after the Alliance was created. Their commitment has stretched from generation to generation. This commitment has called them to examine the intersection of Baptist identity, preaching liberation, and embodiment of their call. Each story is unique and intersectional with other stories. Through the particularity of their stories, we learn of certain universal aspects of women in Baptist life.

We all can learn something from this powerful song that Mary sang in the Gospel of Luke. Do we view ourselves with the same power that Mary viewed herself? Do we claim our full identities—the ones created by God—and let them sing freely? What song is God inviting us to proclaim from right where we stand?

There's so much to unpack in a study of the Magnificat, and this study is one that can aid you, your church, or your small group as you begin to do just that.

Over the course of the study, you'll take a brief journey through the history of the Alliance of Baptists. (This section follows the introduction as an optional part of the study. It informs each woman's story and the context of their ministries.) Then you'll study the Magnificat yourself and talk about its impact on you and what story you want to proclaim. Finally, we'll hear from the six women themselves, who have wrestled with this text and identify with it.

Through it all we'll hear voices from the ones who went before us, highlighted alongside the weekly readings, have daily prayers of reflection, and engage with the ideas of liberation, power, and proclamation. The sermons, which follow the stories of each preacher, are all on the same texts, yet each one shares a unique perspective, highlighting different areas of the text for further enlightenment.

After the body of the weekly study, you'll find a few items to help you reflect throughout the week:

This Week: A suggested activity to work on through the week. This could be a written exercise, a contemplative practice, or a prayer.

Questions for Reflection and Discussion: Starter questions are at the end of each chapter for personal or group reflection. See where the Spirit takes you!

Further Study: Some weeks include a section that invites you to experience other biblical texts, songs, and stories that take us to a deeper engagement with the Magnificat.

At the end of the book, you will find the following appendices:

Leader's Guide: A suggested teaching plan is outlined for a group study for each of the weeks.

Sermon Series and Worship Planning: Following the songs of Luke is a natural Advent Christmas sermon series. Suggested texts, titles, calls to worship, hymns, and themes follow.

Bibliography: Additional texts that were consulted, quoted, and read can all provide more background on the Magnificat, Baptist life, and women in ministry.

Endnotes

[1] Judith Bledsoe Bailey, *Strength for the Journey: Feminist Theology and Baptist Women Pastors* (Richmond: Center for Baptist Heritage and Studies, 2015), 176–177.

[2] Pam Durso and Kevin Pranato, "Baptist Women in Ministry: State of Women in Baptist Life Report 2015" (paper presented at the annual meeting of Baptist Women in Ministry, Winston-Salem, June 26, 2016).

Anticipation: Context & History of the Alliance of Baptists

Upon the birth of the Alliance of Baptists, the support of women in ministry emerged as one of its key emphases. The covenant of the Alliance of Baptists would serve as the guiding document, which both explored Baptist distinctives or freedoms and affirmed women who preached.

These Baptist freedoms would be what women pointed to and connected with as they considered their calls to preach. Over the course of Baptist history, the term *Baptist distinctives* emerged as one way to describe the tenets of what it means to be Baptist. Soul freedom, religious liberty, priesthood of the believer, autonomy of the local church, and believer's baptism are distinguishing characteristics held by Baptists in England in the early seventeenth century.[1]

However, as Baptist historian Bill Leonard points out, trying to narrow down these distinctives or define into any unifying type of consensus is nearly impossible: "From their beginnings in seventeenth-century Europe, Baptists have demonstrated beliefs and practices so diverse as to make it difficult to compile a consistent list of distinctives applicable to all segments of the movement at time."[2] This idea of existing within a plurality of Baptist opinions has always functioned as a strength for Baptists and a place for conversation and dissent.

The Alliance of Baptists formed as a prophetic voice in Baptist life in 1987 with thirty-three individual founders—thirty men and three women. In its earliest days the movement self-identified as an "Exodus people singing a liberation song." As the organization formed, they sought justice and core Baptist liberating freedoms as they left and, in some cases, were forced to leave the SBC.

The SBC was going through what Baptists who left would call "the fundamentalist takeover." From the late 1970s to the early 1990s, the operating procedures and theology of the SBC swung quickly to the right. As Alliance founder Alan Neely would say, "History will record, I believe, that this was a struggle for the soul of what it means to be Baptist."[3]

SBC annual meetings during this period were characterized by the silencing of women, votes happening in secret, and maneuvering to elect only those from the fundamentalist group. Southern Baptist seminaries were firing female faculty, forcing professors to sign statements of faith, and not allowing female students to take preaching classes.

The issue of women in ministry and autonomy of the local church became the two most discussed issues at the time. Women had been ordained within Southern Baptist churches since Addie Davis at Watts Street Baptist Church, Durham, North Carolina, in 1964. What has continued to be common in Baptist life is that although Davis was ordained in an SBC church, she had to go to the American Baptist Churches USA to find a pastoral position in Vermont.[4]

At the formation of the Alliance of Baptists, women were removed from roles of leadership within the SBC, including denominational leadership, some churches, and seminaries.[5] The issue of Baptist identity for women clergy was on the forefront of Baptist-wide discussions and had immediate, hard-hitting ramifications for those involved. This attention to women and women's bodies being excluded from the pulpit and pastoral roles echoes through the generations of Baptist life and impacts the awareness of the younger generation's calling.

These theological and ecclesial issues, like autonomy of the local church, priesthood of the believer, and soul freedom had far-ranging impacts on the state of Baptist life and women ministers. Birthed from schism and what many would call an oppressive regime of the SBC, members of the Alliance did and sometimes continue to identify as "an exodus people, a justice people, a movement people."[6]

The founders agreed that the Alliance needed a guiding document of principles, and what came to be was the covenant. The founders felt the need to sing truth to power—echoing the tradition of the prophet Mary. The Alliance of Baptists covenant, as adopted in 1987, reads:

> In a time when historic Baptist principles, freedoms, and traditions need a clear voice, and in our personal and corporate response to the call of God in Jesus Christ to be

disciples and servants in the world, we commit ourselves to:

1) The freedom of the individual, led by God's Spirit within the family of faith, to read and interpret the Scriptures, relying on the historical understanding by the church and on the best methods of modern biblical study;

2) The freedom of the local church under the authority of Jesus Christ to shape its own life and mission, call its own leadership, and ordain whom it perceives as gifted for ministry, male or female;

3) The larger body of Jesus Christ, expressed in various Christian traditions, and to a cooperation with believers everywhere in giving full expression to the Gospel;

4) The servant role of leadership within the church, following the model of our Servant Lord, and to full partnership of all of God's people in mission and ministry;

5) Theological education in congregations, colleges, and seminaries characterized by reverence for biblical authority and respect for open inquiry and responsible scholarship;

6) The proclamation of the Good News of Jesus Christ and the calling of God to all peoples to repentance and faith, reconciliation and hope, social and economic justice;

7) The principle of a free church in a free state and the opposition to any effort either by church or state to use the other for its own purposes.[7]

Anne Thomas Neil, long-time member of the Alliance, former SBC missionary, and proponent of women in ministry, said upon reading the covenant, "I read these seven principles and then I read them again. I knew I had been waiting since my early childhood for this moment.

To be honest, I never expected to see the formation of such a community of faith in my lifetime."[8]

As the story goes, a subcommittee drafted the covenant, and when brought to the founders, only three words were changed in the entire document. The membership heartily approved it at the annual meeting.[9] This risk of leaving their Baptist home and all that was familiar—because of principles—paved the way for the concept of taking risks to be a huge theme through the life of the Alliance.

One of the Alliance founders, Walker Knight of Atlanta, Georgia, said, "The Alliance formed around principles and has remained principle focused. And if we don't remain principle focused, then there's no reason to exist."[10] These principles have been the guide for the organization throughout its thirty-plus years. Andrew Gardner writes in *Reimagining Zion*,

> This organization created a space for theologically marginalized Baptists to participate and thrive in denominational life. The organization's history is permeated with an inclusiveness and hospitality that reaches out in partnership to disenfranchised female ministers, members of the gay, lesbian, bisexual and transgender (LGBT) community, radical Baptists in Cuba, after-school programs on the South Side of Chicago, and many more.[11]

The inclusiveness and hospitality from the birth of the organization connected with marginalized Baptist women who were searching for a place to be ordained and serve as ministers. Although the issue of women's ordination was supported and even one of the most energizing reasons behind the creation of the Alliance, the day-to-day work of supporting women was not always evident. In the early days there were discussions about how to support women fully and not use them "as a prop upon which the Alliance stood."[12]

Nancy Hastings Sehested and Susan Lockwood, two Alliance founders, were key in this move toward equity within the Alliance. They pursued discussions with the board of directors, led workshops at the annual gathering, and ensured that women were always in leadership in worship and preaching situations. Their faithfulness and dedication, alongside Anne Thomas Neil and many others, ensured that women in ministry, and all women, were truly a valued and supported part of the Alliance of Baptists.

This Week

In our world today, what kind of birthing is needed by people of faith? What is calling to you as an area where you or your church needs to focus? Consider what is stirring within you to be born in the world. Write a prayer that guides you for the week.

Questions for Discussion and Reflection

1. Have you heard of the Alliance of Baptists?

2. What's your relationship to this Baptist history? How does the history and discussion about the formation of this new Baptist group in 1987 sit with you?

3. Whether you or your church are members of the Alliance of Baptists, what sounds like good news to you in the covenant? What pieces need updating or more explanation for you? How would you expand it?

4. Have you ever worked on the creation of a covenant?

5. Do any of these stories about formation speak to you? What have you helped to birth into the world at a critical time? Revisit that place and time. What was going on? Who was alongside you? Who was missing? How was God moving in you and the world?

Endnotes

[1] Bill J. Leonard, *Baptist Ways: A History* (Valley Forge: Judson Press, 2003), 1.

[2] Ibid.

[3] Alan Neely, *Being Baptist Means Freedom* (Charlotte: Southern Baptist Alliance, 1988), vi.

[4] Sarah Frances Anders, "Tracing Past and Present," in *The New Has Come*, ed. Anne Thomas Neil (Washington: Southern Baptist Alliance, 1989), 18.

[5] Ibid., 17–18.

[6] Keith Menhinick, "My Kind of People," *Alliance of Baptists*, April 27, 2015, accessed January 6, 2017, https://allianceofbaptists.org/PCP/alliance_blog_detail/aobgathering-my-kind-of-people-by-keith-a.-menhinick.

[7] "Covenant," last modified April 2013, *Alliance of Baptists,* accessed October 1, 2018, https://allianceofbaptists.org/about/covenant-mission.

[8] Andrew Gardner, *Reimagining Zion: A History of the Alliance of Baptists* (Macon: Nurturing Faith, *2015*), *42.*

[9] Ibid., 41.

[10] Paula Clayton Dempsey (director of partnership relations, Alliance of Baptists), discussion with the author, November 1, 2014.

[11] Gardner, 1.

[12] Ibid., 61.

WEEK ONE
Hope: You and the Magnificat

A prayer for this week:

God,
We magnify your name, and we rejoice in you, O Christ our Savior. You have looked upon the lowliness of all of us and have seen our goodness that you created. Surely, from all generations we will be called blessed because we know you. You have done great things for us, O Prince of Peace, and we will always proclaim your name to the whole earth.

You have brought down the powerful from their thrones, and we have seen the lowly lifted up in your hope, peace, joy, and love. God, we beg you to make yourself known in our world this day. Lift up the lowly, fill the hungry with good things, and remember your people with your mercy and loving kindness. We pray for your presence with those who are grieving today. For the hearts that are heaving the sobs that come so easily now, be present with them.

God, we confess all these things, and we join Mary in her song of justice-love. We sing that you are the one who made all things, redeems all things, and sustains all things. We join Mary as she sings, and yet we know we are called to action. Push us outside our comfort zones to walk alongside our neighbors and speak out against injustice for the poor and the oppressed. Show us your peace in a new way.

We wait for you, and as we wait, we know that you are here in this moment and yet you are coming still. So we wait and hope. Come, Lord Jesus; come quickly. Amen.

Bible Study on the Magnificat

Luke 1

^{39}In those days Mary set out and went with haste to a Judean town in the hill country, ^{40}where she entered the house of Zechariah and greeted Elizabeth. ^{41}When

Elizabeth heard Mary's greeting, the child leaped in her womb. And Elizabeth was filled with the Holy Spirit ⁴²and exclaimed with a loud cry, "Blessed are you among women, and blessed is the fruit of your womb. ⁴³And why has this happened to me, that the mother of my Lord comes to me? ⁴⁴For as soon as I heard the sound of your greeting, the child in my womb leaped for joy. ⁴⁵And blessed is she who believed that there would be a fulfillment of what was spoken to her by the Lord."

⁴⁶And Mary said,
"My soul magnifies the Lord,
⁴⁷and my spirit rejoices in God my Savior,
⁴⁸for he has looked with favor on the lowliness of his servant. Surely, from now on all generations will call me blessed;
⁴⁹for the Mighty One has done great things for me, and holy is his name.
⁵⁰His mercy is for those who fear him from generation to generation.
⁵¹He has shown strength with his arm; he has scattered the proud in the thoughts of their hearts.
⁵²He has brought down the powerful from their thrones, and lifted up the lowly;
⁵³he has filled the hungry with good things, and sent the rich away empty.
⁵⁴He has helped his servant Israel, in remembrance of his mercy,
⁵⁵according to the promise he made to our ancestors, to Abraham and to his descendants forever."
⁵⁶And Mary remained with her about three months and then returned to her home.

This is our text for this study—a short seventeen verses in which we will immerse ourselves and that we will hold up like a jewel so we catch the light from all sides.

The Gospel of Luke is interested in telling the story of the early days of Jesus, just like Matthew is. But Luke gives attention and voice to Mary, Elizabeth, and other women. Luke's Gospel was most likely written by a Gentile, a non-Jew, and Luke loves to include the least likely people in his stories. He loves telling the stories of the poor, the outcast, the downtrodden—the ones normally excluded from the stage.

He is also deeply concerned with sharing the news that the spirit of God is at work in the world. Several times throughout his Gospel, he mentions that the spirit of the Lord anointed this person or that person and rested upon them.

Luke gives us a Gospel unlike any other. For much of it, women are central characters. In the Gospel of Matthew, Mary is mute. Mark's Gospel shows little attention to Mary; nothing from the birth narrative is mentioned, and she only shows up with Jesus's brothers in chapter 3.[1]

But Luke is attentive to Mary. In fact, in these beginning chapters Elizabeth and Mary will announce the coming of the Christ child, and at the end of Luke's Gospel, Mary Magdalene will run, out of breath, to proclaim that he is risen. Luke wants us to know this is the story of good news for all people, and he is determined to give voice to the voiceless.[2]

Mary has just been visited by Gabriel, and she accepts this great responsibility of bringing Jesus into the world. The child growing within her will embody the good news in the same way she does—proclaiming it to all and then some.

As the nerves of the pregnancy set in, we can imagine that Mary needed some space to breathe as she set off to visit her cousin Elizabeth, who was also pregnant—miraculously in her advanced maternal age—with John the Baptist. These two women have been depicted throughout history as an example of the strength of women's relationships. Elizabeth and Mary were the only ones who could understand each other and their circumstances. Elizabeth's pregnancy came as a surprise to everyone—especially to her and to her husband, Zechariah, who was a priest.

During one of Zechariah's days at the temple, he went into the holy of holies to make an offering. While inside, the angel Gabriel (yes, the same Gabriel) showed up. In a type-scene that you might recognize, Zechariah was told that he and his wife, who were both around eighty, would be having a baby and this baby was to be named John. A laugh heard across the centuries, starting with Sarah and finishing with Zechariah, was only stifled by his utter disbelief. I guess Gabriel and God expected more from Zechariah than to doubt, so God struck him mute for the entirety of Elizabeth's pregnancy and the first week of his son's life.

Zechariah—the priest, the preacher, the one with all the privilege in the land—was silenced for nine months while Elizabeth and Mary—two without standing, waddling around pregnant with no privilege or rights—were the ones to proclaim the good news of God during that time.

This is where our passage from Luke begins. Zechariah is silent, and Elizabeth and Mary are humming lullabies and proclaiming the fullness of God's love from right where they stand. Luke encourages us to join the scene with all the detail. Babies are leaping, and two women's souls are jumping with joy.

Elizabeth recognized what was happening here. Mary was welcomed into her home, and some of Mary's worst fears were nullified. Elizabeth welcomed her and called her blessed. Her baby was called "Lord," and Mary's faithfulness was praised.

Mary's immediate reply to Elizabeth is the song we know as the Magnificat. It's Mary's song of praise to God and her song of freedom for her people. It's rich and layered with meaning. Although Elizabeth and Mary are singing their songs to each other, they are in conversation with one another. In the collection of books in our Bible, there are very few places where women speak to one another without the presence of a man. There are even fewer passages where women speak to one another and are not speaking about a man.

As writer Anne Emry said, "Mary gave of herself, of her humanity. Jesus came from her humanity, just as he came from God. It is worth pondering—that God because incarnate in the young mother before God became incarnate in Jesus."[3]

Mary had long known the story of her faith. She is bursting with the news God has given her and that news that she has known her whole life. Mary's song in verses 50–55 is deeply prophetic. Her faithful song is what people will sing for generations to come, and she will be known as blessed. God has shown the power as people are scattered, as the powerful are brought down from their thrones and the lowly are lifted up.

God has filled those who hunger with good things, with life and sustenance, and sent away the ones who are stingy with what they have, the cry of their stomachs reminding them of their lack of generosity. And God has remembered all of God's people in mercy, lavishing grace upon grace in the world.

This is Luke's Gospel, remember, so Mary sings her song as a song of freedom for all people—especially the ones who have been forgotten. She sings it perhaps with her lower lip trembling a little bit because she believes, a little bit because she is scared. She sings it as tears stream down her face because she knows the reality of the cry of the hungry children who surround her in her hometown.

She sings even as she longs for her beloved Palestine to be at peace. She sings it in the midst of scarcity of grain and the abundance of power of the Roman Empire. She sings all of it because, as Barbara Brown Taylor says, Mary is singing ahead of time.[4] Mary sings because she believes even as she lives in the midst of reality. As she sings, she does not abandon the reality of her situation.

Mary sings of the day when all things will be made new. This is the work of a prophet. She is singing the words that comfort the afflicted and afflict the comfortable. She sings our song. Mary sings us a song that lingers in our ears and rests deep down in our bones. Mary sings a song that moves us.

When Mary opens her mouth to sing, she sings of an upside-down, inside-out kingdom of God. She sings of what the world could be when we look at it through the eyes and promises of God.

The Magnificat and the power of song always reminds me of the time I traveled to New York City with my clergy group as part of a grant we received for continuing education. Our work on this trip was to look for the light in the darkness, to pay attention to the places where light shone even as the darkness was trying to drown it out.

We visited the 9-11 memorial and saw the sunshine flickering on the water and creating hope-filled drops of water. We visited a Broadway production and listened as the commentary on religious culture looked dark but actually ended with a light-filled moment of redemption.

But I think, without a doubt, the most moving stop on our trip was to the Cloisters, which is part of the Metropolitan Museum of Art.

The Cloisters is not located in the Central Park location of the Met; instead it sits atop a hill, looking over the river, leading you to almost forget you are in the city altogether.

We climbed the hill and went into the museum, which recreated medieval monasteries with materials and works of art from all over Europe. As we walked in, we started to hear this music, which inexplicably drew us in. Artist Janet Cardiff had created a performance art installation. All around the room were speakers. Over the course of 14 minutes, the composition by Thomas Tallis played the forty-part motet *Spem in alium numquam habui* and we were spellbound.

People were standing like statues, with eyes closed and in what appeared to be complete peace, in front of speakers. We, too, froze immediately, for we were all participants in Tallis's song of hope. People were standing in complete awe as the music washed over them. I couldn't help but think of the Magnificat in that moment.

The space was sacred. The music was sacred. The music was moving people in a way that only those songs that meet us in deep places do. Mary's prophetic song is like that—singing about all of our deepest hopes, all of God's deepest hopes. Mary is participating in the song of salvation.

But the beauty of Mary's song is that we now can sing it all together. When we get to the line that I have trouble believing in, all I do is look around and see someone else singing it for me. And when we get to the part where you have trouble believing, look around and see the rest of us singing it for you.

We sing Mary's song with joy because now it is ours to sing—we are all the mothers of God, birthing God's love into a world desperate for it. Nancy Rockwell said, "The work of prophecy is physical work: bearing God into a weary and unwelcoming world."[5] We wait with an Advent pause—one that connects all time and space. We wait, and if we listen carefully, we can hear the good news of God leaping off the lips of Mary and off our lips into a broken, hurting world.

As you finish up this reflection on this passage from Luke, receive these parting words: "May your souls magnify the Lord and your spirits rejoice in God your Savior. For God has looked with favor on you, and all generations will call you blessed. For the Mighty One has done great things for you."

This Week

Tell your own story in light of this text. What would your song be—a song of praise, protest, lament, hope? All of the above? Write or illustrate that song, or at least begin humming the melody that is bubbling up in your soul. What sounds like good news to you?

Questions for Reflection and Discussion

1. How do you think Mary felt when she approached Elizabeth's home?

2. How does Mary's song speak to our world today? How does she point to God's activity in the world?

3. Does this passage from Mary sound like good news to you? Does it seem like an expression of God's abundance in the world?

4. What do you think it meant for Jesus to grow up with a mother like Mary? Do you think he heard this song again in his young life?

5. Have there been songs in your life that influenced you and formed you in faith? Hymns at church? A song your family sang together growing up? A song or chant or protest song that brought you hope? Listen to that song, and see what emerges within you. Do you feel centered? Inspired?

Further Study

Looking back over all of our history, our joint history, our biblical history, it's important to look at some of the places where Mary found inspiration—her foremothers and their songs. Take a look and engage with the stories of Miriam's song in Exodus and Hannah's song in 1 Samuel.

1. What is Miriam singing about in Exodus 15:20–21?

> [20]Then the prophet Miriam, Aaron's sister, took a tambourine in her hand; and all the women went out after her with tambourines and with dancing. [21]And Miriam sang to them:
>
> "Sing to the Lord, for he has triumphed gloriously;
> horse and rider he has thrown into the sea."

2. What is Hannah singing about in 1 Samuel 2:1–10? Do you think Mary found comfort in this song? What do you notice about her words?

Hannah prayed and said,

> "My heart exults in the Lord;
> my strength is exalted in my God.
> My mouth derides my enemies,
> because I rejoice in my victory.
> ² "There is no Holy One like the Lord,
> no one besides you;
> there is no Rock like our God.
> ³ Talk no more so very proudly,
> let not arrogance come from your mouth;
> for the Lord is a God of knowledge,
> and by him actions are weighed.
> ⁴ The bows of the mighty are broken,
> but the feeble gird on strength.
> ⁵ Those who were full have hired themselves out for bread,
> but those who were hungry are fat with spoil.
> The barren has borne seven,
> but she who has many children is forlorn.
> ⁶ The Lord kills and brings to life;
> he brings down to Sheol and raises up.
> ⁷ The Lord makes poor and makes rich;
> he brings low, he also exalts.
> ⁸ He raises up the poor from the dust;
> he lifts the needy from the ash heap,
> to make them sit with princes
> and inherit a seat of honor.
> For the pillars of the earth are the Lord's,
> and on them he has set the world.
>
> ⁹ "He will guard the feet of his faithful ones,
> but the wicked shall be cut off in darkness;
> for not by might does one prevail.
> ¹⁰ The Lord! His adversaries shall be shattered;
> the Most High will thunder in heaven.

> The Lord will judge the ends of the earth;
> he will give strength to his king,
> and exalt the power of his anointed."

3. What do you hear emerging from those songs from Miriam and Hannah? This presents an arc from the exodus to the early days of Israel to Mary and the birth of Jesus. What themes emerge? What seems like good news to you?

4. Imagine Mary singing her song as Jesus was growing up around their home. Do you think it influenced him? Read Luke 4:16–21 as Jesus enters the synagogue, and take a look at what he says. Does the language sound familiar?

> [16] When he came to Nazareth, where he had been brought up, he went to the synagogue on the sabbath day, as was his custom. He stood up to read, [17] and the scroll of the prophet Isaiah was given to him. He unrolled the scroll and found the place where it was written:
>
> [18] "The Spirit of the Lord is upon me,
> because he has anointed me
> to bring good news to the poor.
> He has sent me to proclaim release to the captives
> and recovery of sight to the blind,
> to let the oppressed go free,
> [19] to proclaim the year of the Lord's favor."
> [20] And he rolled up the scroll, gave it back to the attendant, and sat down. The eyes of all in the synagogue were fixed on him. [21] Then he began to say to them, "Today this scripture has been fulfilled in your hearing."

Endnotes

[1] James F. Kay, "Mary's Song—and Ours," *Christian Century* (December 10, 1997), 1157.

[2] Alyce M. McKenzie, "Blessed Are We," *Edgy Exegesis* (May 31, 2012).

[3] Anne Emry, "The Song of Mary," *Sacred Story* (December 21, 2012).

⁴ Barbara Brown Taylor, "Singing Ahead of Time," *Home By Another Way.* (Cowley Publications:, Plymouth, UK, 1999), 15.

⁵ Nancy Rockwell, "No More Lying About Mary," *Patheos (December 3, 2015).*

WEEK TWO
Peace

This week begins three weeks of reading the stories of women preachers, their engagement with Mary and the Magnificat, their sermons, and their connection to being Baptist, particularly of the Alliance of Baptists variety. We begin with the stories of Rev. Nancy Hastings Sehested and Rev. Dr. Isabel Docampo. Questions for discussion and reflection follow both women's stories and sermons.

Rev. Nancy Hastings Sehested
Co-pastor, Circle of Mercy Church, Asheville, NC

Nancy Hastings Sehested, one of the founders of the Alliance of Baptists, speaks to the promise of God's presence and of God's calling on the lives of women. Sehested was there from the very moment of conception of this organization we now refer to as "the Alliance" and served as president from 1996–1998. Remembering the days of the schism from the SBC and the foundation of the Alliance, she explained, "We were a renegade group that felt disenfranchised. We were meeting in small groups all over the place—in gatherings around SBC annual meetings and in late-night meetings. The seeds for the Alliance started in those gatherings where we felt like we were exiles."[2]

As one of the thirty-three founders, three of whom were women, Sehested helped to create the covenant. As she recalls, it was not easy in the beginning to move on the issue of women in ministry.

> Expect resistance, but do not let that hinder you from fully claiming whom God has called you to be. Remember we are able to move forward because there have been many women who have sacrificed before us. We don't know all their names, but we know they paved the way. Unheralded women continue to create the space to sing forth our songs of courage and hope with Mary.[1]

The Alliance affirmed women in ministry, but some of the founders didn't see the need to have it stated in the covenant: "That line about the mutual partnership of women and men was born out of that historical moment. Even men who were ordaining women would say things like, 'What, don't you trust us? Do we really need to include this in the covenant?'"[3]

Nancy Hastings Sehested grew up in a Baptist family, so "Baptist" was the name that happened to be hers. Although Baptist life is full of scoundrels and saints, she still felt that what was near and dear to her and her identity were the Baptist distinctives of soul freedom and priesthood of the believer.

Her devotion to the Bible and the stories therein helped her claim her identity: "The centrality of the Bible is that we claim the story. I caught the story growing up. I've given up on the church a few times, but I've never given up on the story. I caught the story, and the story caught me."[4] Being caught up in the wildness and vastness of the story also gave her the powerful understanding about missions: "We give ourselves sacrificially in a servant role to those who are not people of privilege and power."[5] That's part of her understanding of the good news, laced with understandings from the Gospel of Luke: "I joined the other founders in longing to be a part of a Baptist movement for peace and justice, one that clearly claimed our servant role in bringing good news to those who are poor."[6]

In 1978 she graduated from Union Theological Seminary in New York. She knew she wanted to pastor but was unsure where she might find a church that would call a woman. She was ordained in 1981 at Oakhurst Baptist Church, Decatur, Georgia, and preached there regularly. She said, "At first it felt awkward to stand in the pulpit to preach. It was strange for all of us, really. Cultural conditioning can do that to us. However, it was also a historical moment, and women were finding their way into pulpits around the country. Even in the awkwardness, it felt right, in a justice sense."[7]

For Sehested it was a leap of courage just to stand in the pulpit. She was called to pastor Prescott Memorial Baptist Church, Memphis, Tennessee, in 1987. While there, she began to hone her preaching voice. She was greatly affirmed by the congregation even though they suffered during the takeover of the SBC. She recalls little girls asking her if boys could preach, as their new model in ministry was a woman. She also remembers that if she preached a particularly tough passage—such as from the prophet Jeremiah—she would receive chicken casseroles the next week because people thought she needed to be cheered up. They were not accustomed to hearing a woman offer the challenging words of a biblical prophet. Soothing words were more the social norm for the public words from women.

Nancy Hastings Sehested has always felt a connection with Mary and the Magnificat and has preached many sermons in her career on the Lukan passage. She has likened the context of Mary's song to herself, the church, and the Alliance of Baptists. Throughout her career she witnessed various power dynamics in the church and in society. People sometimes think of Mary as powerless; she lived in a violent and hostile world, and yet she courageously lived her call with all that was within her.[8] In her earliest sermons Sehested felt kinship with Mary, a young woman stepping up against powerful forces resistant to God's vision. But she lived into the hope every time she stepped into a pulpit or pastoral role.

Mary calls Sehested back to herself.

There have been times when she has questioned her Baptist identity. She wondered where else she could go, but everywhere she looked, obstacles for women in ministry existed: "Throughout my years of ministry, the most hateful and hostile words that have come my way have been from Baptists. But also some of the most loving, courageous, beautiful people that I know have been Baptist."[9] The Alliance of Baptists has always been small and, at times, has struggled with its size. Sehested reflects, "The Alliance has always been small and yet always had power. What does that look like when we feel inadequate? It looks like Alliance people who are incarnating God's radical story of love, like Mary. It looks like gospel to me."[10]

In her sermon on the Magnificat, "Hopes and Fears," from December 21, 2014, at Circle of Mercy, Sehested preached,

> The hopes and fears of all the years burst forth in this song. Mary discovered that she mattered to God. Us too? Just when we think that our tiny life could not possibly matter in the ways that might matter against the horrors of Herod times, the Mischief-Maker shows up with divine design to give us a part to play. Our faith is not a message until it's an experience. It is first birthed in us through

body and soul. Mary's "yes" was a journey of love incarnated in the mess and miracle of a Herod world. Our hope is still for a world without the horrors of Herod. Such a hope requires all the love that is within us. God's still in the birthing room, and all's wild with the world.[11]

Nancy Hastings Sehested's "yes" helped birth the Alliance of Baptists and generations of Baptist women preachers.

Her benediction to you is this: "The surprises of God's spirit are still bringing new life amid the miracle and mess of it all, and we are bodying forth the good news of God's transforming love."

"Hopes and Fears"

A sermon preached by Rev. Nancy Hastings Sehested at Circle of Mercy Congregation, Asheville, North Carolina on December 21, 2014

The stories this time of year are so familiar that we might be lulled into the idea that they are tame and reasonable. There is nothing much tame in these stories, in spite of the fact that Luke begins his storytelling to *most excellent Theophilus, "friend of God"* by giving a really good reason for it all: *I decided after investigating everything carefully from the very first, to write an orderly account for you* (Luke 1:3). Really, Luke? After investigating everything carefully, this is your orderly account? Aren't you glad he told us?

Luke expected us to know quite a bit about the backdrop of the stories. His very first line after his introduction: *In the days of King Herod of Judea.*

Oh, most excellent Theophilus-es, honorable friends of God, if we miss this opening, we miss the meaning. We might miss the divine mischief-making in the mayhem. It's time to put Herod back in Christmas. Not because we need any more Herods, but because it reveals that the sweet manger was placed in the midst of grave danger.

In the days of King Herod, in the days when innocents were being killed, children were being killed.

In the days of King Herod, a census was devised to document the undocumented for government control, as well as to ensure taxation of the most vulnerable ones.

In the days of King Herod, the lives of the people without power mattered little to those who ruled the land.

In the days of King Herod, hunger was common, shelter was scarce, and people lived in fear for their lives and the lives of their children.

So now we know for certain those days are our days. This story is our story.

The story unfolds not in the palaces of power but in tiny places, places hardly worth a mention. They were places where the "important" stuff usually didn't happen, like in a sanctuary, in a hill country, in a house in Nazareth, in a town of Bethlehem, in a manger, in the fields. And into those small places walked people easily ignored and dismissed, like priests, peasants, animals, innkeepers, babies, and shepherds. Smallish things happened—things you might expect to hear around a campfire or a dinner table or a church retreat.

An elderly priest lost his voice when his wife turned up pregnant. The priest's pregnant wife invited her shamed teenage pregnant cousin into her house for sanctuary. The priest's wife gave birth to a baby who was named one of the most common names in the baby scrolls of those times, John.

Then the young pregnant girl found her voice and discovered she had a talent for song-writing and wrote a song for the ages. The young teen's fiancé decided not to leave her but stayed with her through the whole labor and delivery as well as through the singing of a caroling group of shepherds. And a baby was born. A baby.

Fascinating story but not earth-shattering, except for those angels—the messengers—who had the ability to pop up out of nowhere to give a message to nobodies and to frighten already frightened people.

The messengers stepped into the threshold places, between what is seen and unseen, between what can be calculated and what can be experienced. They offered an invitation to make a journey with the Spirit. They showed up during the worst of times, just when no one thought anything could be done, and their message was, "God is busy, busy, busy. God is having the time of her life, and you're invited to be part of it."

Mary was troubled with the message. The angel Gabriel offered a slim shred of assurance: "Don't be afraid." Then the messenger made attempts to explain things, but his message showed some room for improvement.

He said, "God's spirit is popping up all over the place, and one of the designated sights is your body. God-life will be birthed through you.

You're going to have a baby! Yes, that's right. Oh, don't thank me. Thank the Holy Dreamer. She thought this one up. I'm just the messenger."

The language of the angel was particular and scandalous: "This baby will be great. The son of the Most High. The son of God." It was language used for the emperor of the land—you know the one—Caesar Augustus.

God was scheming up a radical plan of counter-insurgency, a divine gift of power that was embedded in the tiny womb of a woman of seeming insignificance. Mary's question of "How can this be?" was more a question of theology than biology. What was God up to? And with her?

We stand beside Mary as astonished as she is. God's spirit can be birthed through us—unlikely us. God becomes tiny hands and feet and face. God becomes a needy, squalling baby.

The angel left God's calling card: "Nothing is impossible with God."

And with that, Mary courageously said yes to what she could not fully comprehend, any more than we can understand how our seemingly ordinariness can become extraordinary holy creations. Mary went with haste to the hill country to see her cousin Elizabeth.

Elizabeth could've said, "Oh, no! This is a total disaster!" She could've shunned her. She could've said, "You've brought shame on this family." She could've rebuked her, humiliated her, dismissed her.

But Elizabeth's body spoke up even before her words could utter a sound. Her body told the truth before her lips had a chance to voice it. Her own baby leapt in her womb. There was life stirring in her dark womb where she never imagined such an impossible possibility at her age. She welcomed Mary. She blessed Mary.

And in such an embrace another miracle came forth. A song burst out of Mary—song of joy and praise, oh yes—but a song that placed this miracle smack in the middle of the King Herod world. She said something like this:

> I'm overflowing with thanks to God.
> I'm dancing to the song of God.
> God chose me—of all people.
> I'm blessed beyond words.
> God has done great things for me. Just look at me!
> God's mercy is endless.
> I hope my baby knows such mercy.

> I hope my baby knows a world full of God's creating,
> Where the high and mighty proud are put in their place—
> their place right alongside all of us.
> I hope my baby knows a world where tyrants and terrorists become harmless
> And those whose lives never mattered, all matter.
> I hope my baby knows a world where the hungry have a taste of plenty
> And the overstuffed know the gnaw of hunger.
> I hope my baby knows a world where mercies pile higher than cruelties
> And where the promise of peace cascades through every generation.

The hopes and fears of all the years burst forth in this song. Mary discovered that she mattered to God. Us too? Just when we think that our tiny life could not possibly matter in the ways that might matter against the horrors of Herod times, the Mischief-Maker shows up with divine design to give us a part to play.

Our faith is not a message until it's an experience. It is first birthed in us through body and soul. Mary's yes was a journey of love incarnated in the mess and miracle of a Herod world.

(Note: I picked up and held a small globe in one hand and a baby in the other hand for the final words of the sermon.)

Our hope is still for a world without the horrors of Herod. Such a hope requires all the love that is within us. God's still in the birthing room, and all's wild with the world.

"Magnify the Lord"

A sermon preached by Rev. Nancy Hastings Sehested at Circle of Mercy Congregation, Asheville, North Carolina on December 19, 2010

Night falls. Darkness surrounds us. Fear rises. The voices held back in the light of day emerge. Darkness closes in around us. Ever notice how much darkness is in the biblical stories of this season? The darkness of uncertainty. The darkness of despair and hopelessness. The darkness of confusion. Who can see clearly?

Out of this darkness a poetic voice is heard, the voice of a young woman who pokes holes in the night sky with her words: *My soul magnifies the Lord, and my spirit rejoices in God my Savior.*

What gave rise to these words in Mary? If we look closely at the story, it comes during her visit with her cousin, a woman she could confide in, a woman who could understand.

Elizabeth knew the long sad darkness of lost dreams. The song of Mary would be appropriate on the lips of Elizabeth, especially since so much of it is the song of Hannah, the song of a barren woman who was given new life. Some of the ancient Latin translations attribute the song to Elizabeth. But in our translation it is bubbling up from Mary. Maybe the poetic words emerged out of the courage experienced from the two women understanding the miracle and magnitude of their situations.

The song begins in personal gratitude. God has chosen Mary, one of low estate, a slave. Then the song moves from the personal to the public. It becomes a revolutionary song.

It is known as the great reversal. The revolution is political, economic, and spiritual. Mercy is given. The mighty are put down. The poor are lifted up. The hungry are filled with food. The rich are sent away empty. It is a revolution. It names our longing for justice. But does it fit fully into our vision for God's reign of peace?

Revolutions revolve. One power gets exchanged with another. Jesus's life and witness of God's reign was far more radical. In Jesus's vision no one goes hungry. No one goes away empty. Power is transformed, not just rearranged. How does our soul magnify this Holy One of such a topsy-turvy world?

Night falls. Darkness surrounds us. Where is the light of hope? Luke tells the story with fear and terror and angels on every page, with the hope of Christ birthed in the midst of a dangerous world.

Matthew describes the darkness within dreaded and dire situations. Yet the writer places dreams in the dark that bring hope and stars that guide in the night.

John gives us a poetic rendering of Jesus's beginnings without a story: *In the beginning was the word, and the word was with God, and the word… in him was life, and the life was the light of all people. The light shines in the darkness, and the darkness has not overcome it.*

In Zechariah's song at the birth of John, *light will be given to those who sit in darkness.* The light shone for the shepherds on the hillside.

In our hemisphere Jesus's birth is celebrated in winter, around the time of the winter solstice, the birthday of the sun.

Vaclav Havel, who was once a political prisoner, was asked about hope. He answered with these words:

> I should probably say first that the kind of hope I often think about (especially in situations that are particularly hopeless, such as prison), I understand above all as a state of mind, not a state of the world. Either we have hope within us or we don't; it is a dimension of the soul, and it's not essentially dependent on some particular observation of the world or estimate of the situation. Hope…is an orientation of the heart; it transcends the world that is immediately experienced, and is anchored somewhere beyond the world's horizons…. I think the deepest and most important form of hope, the only one that can keep us above water and urges us to good works, and the only true source of the breathtaking dimensions of the human spirit and its efforts, is something we get, as it were, from "elsewhere."

On my first spelunking adventure I learned quickly in the cave of complete darkness that eyes can't adjust because there is no light getting in. The only light available was the light we brought with us.

I work in a dark place called prison. My light can grow dim at times. This morning's worship service at the prison chapel was an example. Four correctional officers walked into the worship service while I was preaching. Inmates shifted uncomfortably in their chairs. I didn't know the problem, but I knew something was going on. Maybe there was a suspicion that drugs were being slipped from one pocket to another. Or maybe notes were being passed from one hand to another about an upcoming fight. I stepped up my preaching efforts, increased my volume, made sweeping gestures with my arms while telling the inmates about God's light that shines in the darkness. I spoke passionately about Jesus as the Prince of

Peace. I think it was one of my better sermons. I'm sorry you missed it. Then I ended the service early with a prayer for peace.

As the inmates left the chapel, a fight broke out in the hallway. The officers were ready with handcuffs and pepper spray. Thankfully there were no serious injuries. But after all was restored to calm and I prepared to leave the chapel, I thought of my inadequacy, my ineffectiveness. Nothing says failure for a preacher than preaching on peace and a fight breaking out immediately.

Night falls. Darkness surrounds us. And yet—and yet—we lift our voices and pray with Mary: *My soul magnifies the Lord, and my spirit rejoices in God my Redeemer, my saving grace.*

The light of the world begins with life in the darkness of the womb.

The light of the world does not end the darkness, but it gives a different dimension to it. It changes it. It casts a new light on it.

Last summer I walked up the sidewalk to the entryway of the maximum-security unit. I passed the green grass and the blooming impatiens. An inmate from the minimum-security prison jumped off the lawnmower and scooped up a handful of grass clippings. He held it out to me, saying, "Chap, can you help?" Nestled in his hand was a baby bird. "We need to save it," he pleaded. "Okay," I said. "Let's do what we can."

Don't we want to prevent all of life's vulnerable ones from being mowed down from inhumanity and cruelty and dangers and disappointments? We do what we can.

The inmate placed the bird as far back into a bush as possible. I knelt down to form a barrier between the bush and the mower. The inmate zoomed the mower in front of us. I yelled at the bird to stop hopping. Please stay in the womb of safety, little bird. Stay there, little one.

But the bird did not heed my warning. It hopped and hopped. I could not stop it. It was instinctively drawn from the darkness into the light. It jumped out of the bushes into harm's way within a second of missing the mower blades. It made it. The inmate and I clapped our hands and shouted hallelujahs.

God chose a vulnerable young woman to birth a vulnerable baby to live in the darkness of this world and bear forth the light of love. The light beckons us still.

My soul magnifies the Lord, and my spirit rejoices in God my Savior.

Rev. Dr. Isabel Docampo

Associate director of the intern program; professor of supervised ministry, Perkins School of Theology at Southern Methodist University, Dallas, Texas

Isabel Docampo remembers typically being the only woman in her preaching classes in the early 1980s at the Southern Baptist Theological Seminary in Louisville, Kentucky. At that time women were still welcome to take preaching classes, but fewer and fewer women were signing up. In her undergraduate work there were only three women in the biblical studies program at Louisiana College.

Growing up in Louisiana with parents who emigrated from Cuba, Isabel was always aware of her identity and how she never quite felt at home where she was. As a little girl whose parents didn't speak English, struggled to provide a home and navigate the culture, she was ever aware of how she was often seen as an outsider in the United States. Her father was functionally illiterate, and her mother worked hard to get her GED.

> Mary was speaking to the way religion has been co-opted by the Roman Empire. Religion had become institutionalized and oppressive to many. Mary gives us a moment in time where we don't have to accept the status quo. We don't have to live there. God is at work. God does not forget; God is with us. This is an opportunity to reimagine life together and life with God.
>
> —Isabel Docampo[12]

Isabel lived as a bridge-builder between her home and her world, her childhood Baptist church, and herself. Reflecting, she said, "I live a bit uneasy in a world of middle class. One whose life has been spent working with refugees and immigrants, I can always see both sides. My identity doesn't escape me, and being the bridge is tiring. Being of both worlds, but not being of either, is exhausting. Yet it also gives me enormous insights."[13]

After seminary, in 1982 Docampo was appointed as a home missionary for the SBC through the Home Missionary Board (HMB). She returned to Louisiana, working with Latino, Cambodian, and Vietnamese refugees and attending Broadmoor Baptist Church, a predominantly white, English-speaking church in Baton Rouge. She remembers trying to claim her pastoral identity in HMB meetings and that people were constantly trying to strip her of it as the takeover was in full force in Louisiana. Paradoxically, she also experienced enormous support from other leaders and laity that led to her ordination at Broadmoor Baptist Church in 1985. This occurred at the same time women were in the crossfire of the larger battles of women in ministry. A few years after that, she lost her job as the fundamentalists took over the SBC and HMB.

At about the same time, Docampo started receiving mailings and seeing reports in the Louisiana Baptist newspaper about the formation of the Southern Baptist Alliance. The news of this gave her hope, and upon a move to Washington, D.C., she met with Stan Hastey and Jeannette Holt, the directors of the organization. She was piecing together ministry work through a local retirement home, the District of Columbia Baptist Convention, and was always paying attention to what was happening with the Alliance. Docampo's Cuban heritage became connected to the Alliance of Baptists when Stan Hastey asked her to read a letter from the Fraternity of Baptist Churches of Cuba (FIBAC), an Alliance ministry partner. They had just learned at that time that FIBAC wanted the Alliance to come for a visit, and in 1996 she visited with Stan Hastey.

Isabel Docampo has made several partnership trips to Cuba to visit with the FIBAC, and in 1999 Paco Rodes, executive director of FIBAC and pastor of First Baptist Church, Matanzas, invited her to preach in the worship service. Her text that morning was the Magnificat, and she struggled with how to preach it—as a Baptist woman and as a Cuban-American. She had never preached the Magnificat, and she realized she hadn't preached in Spanish in a long time. She was used to preaching in English and realized in that moment that she had work to do surrounding her own identity: "I was handwriting the text and so aware of who the audience was in Matanzas. I was in a communist state. People cannot be motivated to rise up and protest government! I was worried that I might jeopardize the ministry. So I asked Paco what I should do. He said, 'You preach what God has put on your heart; don't worry about us.'"[14]

The Magnificat, in that context in Cuba, was about remembering people who are isolated and caught up in occupation without having to put anyone at risk. She could not mute the power of Mary's song, but she could be smart about nuance.

She saw the text as a personal story of a woman being remembered and chosen, as well as her people being remembered and chosen. "In this Magnificat," Docampo said, "you have liberation personally and communally. In this Magnificat, you have the intersection of oppression and liberation—it speaks of both."[15]

It served as the text at the crux of the moment of identity for Docampo. Always a supporting member of the Alliance of Baptists, Docampo has served on committees, the board of directors, and most recently served as chair of the Annual Gathering Planning Committee in 2016, which met in St. Louis. The theme of the gathering, under her guidance, was "Bearing Courage: Rooted in Hope," highlighting the stories of women and featuring women preachers: Traci Blackmon, Phyllis Trible, and Kyndall Rothaus.

Like most Baptists who lived through the split with the SBC, Isabel Docampo has questioned whether to remain Baptist, concluding, "I'm Baptist. If I'm going to live out this call, this is where I'm going to live it out. I identify with the Alliance of Baptists because it is progressive, and the covenant speaks to me. It best captures my identity and faith values on church polity and doctrine."[16] She works at Southern Methodist University and attends a United Methodist Church and still considers herself Baptist through and through.

To stand in a pulpit as an ordained Baptist woman, Docampo believes she is a witness to freedom and liberation. As she stands there, God is breaking down barriers and weaving freedom with grace. As a Baptist woman she reflects on Mary's voice and her own preaching voice, saying, "Mary is the one that's chosen and given voice. Her voice is strong. This is explicitly about women being chosen, having strength, being blessed, and into the light and anointing of God."[17]

And when Docampo speaks about it, a feminist, mujerista theologian herself, she notes that when Mary sings, she sings as an indigenous person: "The Magnificat helps the indigenous person, the lowest of the low. Mary was a Palestinian Jew. She was indigenous to the land, which was now occupied, and she was at the bottom. In her context an indigenous woman would never have this platform. But Mary did. And she sang of the Divine's faithfulness and of her own power."[18] Mary's power came from knowing her God, her identity, and still singing to the powers of the day.

Isabel Docampo's benediction to you follows: "My soul magnifies the Lord. God has regard for the humble state of this, God's servant. We are endowed with all that God needs. The misogyny cannot take that away from us, and so I exalt my God."

"The Magnificat"

A sermon preached by Rev. Dr. Isabel Docampo at Grace UMC in Dallas, Texas on November 27, 2016

Mary's Magnificat reveals the distorted world that she is living in and how frightening it was. There was hunger in some bellies, strict classification of people as "lowly," and there was suffering. As a young woman Mary lived in a world where men made decisions over her public and private life—who to marry, where to live, what work she would do. As a Jew she lived under occupation by the Roman Empire. At the time the angel Gabriel came, she was about to leave her father's household to enter into her husband's—how would she be welcomed? She had plenty of reasons to stay awake, frightened, long before the angel arrived to tell her not to be afraid.

But of course when the angel appears to her, she is frightened. Quickly, she realizes that the angel comes to her sleepless night so that she doesn't have to be frightened anymore because he tells her that God has not forgotten the promises made and will fulfill them. The angel Gabriel invites her into the work of realizing God's promise that the distorted arrangements of social power don't have to be accepted and that life could be lived differently. Mary says, "Yes! Let's do this!"

When she says this, suddenly this teenage Mary is no longer reduced by the identities given to her: woman, teenager, someone's daughter, someone's wife, Jew, poor, politically powerless. Mary's "yes!" and then her song say a lot about her audacious faith and intellect. It displays how she experiences God's love as overflowing, without limits, and life-giving in its mercy and justice. The Hebrew word for this divine love is *hesed*.

We translate it as "love," but it's a complicated word—it implies justice within unconditional love.

Mary sings out strongly because the angel's visit confirms what she always known in her heart—that God "sees" her! God hears her!

And I wonder if Mary is remembering the story of Hagar in her Hebrew scriptures? Hagar is another young woman who had a meeting with God out of the blue, right when life was literally frightening her to death. I certainly begin to think about that other young girl.

Hagar was Sarah's Egyptian slave that became Abraham's concubine. Hagar is the first person in our Scripture to see and speak with God—*and she does it twice!*—even though she is a slave from a different race and ethnicity. The first time that God appears to her like the angel to Mary, saying, "Do not be afraid!" she was a runaway slave whose wretched life as a sex object to Abraham led her to take her chances with death in the desert. When God appears, like Mary, God promises her a future and a blessing within the difficulty of bearing a son in such oppressive circumstances. God sees her—Hagar—sees her pain, and offers her a future she could not fathom.

The second time Hagar speaks with God is when she and Ishmael, the promised son by Abraham, are dying in the desert and it seems that God has forgotten her—her suffering is so great. This time God speaks and provides water and food. God renews the promise that Ishmael will father a great nation. Hagar, Egyptian slave that she is, nevertheless has a courageous faith that is hopeful—and, like Mary did centuries later, "goes for it" and moves into her future with determination in spite of all the difficulties she has to face. Ishmael does become the father of a great nation.

This story, like Mary's, reveals Hagar's faith in God and how she is so much more than how she is being categorized. It reveals that God hears her pain—her son Ishmael means "God hears." Ishmael is the flesh-and-blood fulfillment of God's blessing. Hagar in the Muslim faith is revered for her fidelity, strength, and resilience. In our Scripture she is an example of how God's love is overflowing and without limits. God's promise to Abraham and Sarah does not mean that God excludes others.

Mary and Hagar are blessed not because they gave birth to two sons, but because of their faithfulness and courage. Their faith allowed them to say "yes" and to do extraordinary things. No wonder Mary sings out, "My soul magnified the Lord! My spirit rejoices in God my savior!"

Can Mary's song be our song? I think so. Mary's Magnificat reveals how our world today is also distorted far from what our Creator intended. It makes us stop and assess if we have accepted the limitations of identity forced upon us and that separate us from one another, if we have accepted a fatalistic view of our current situation as unchangeable. *It is what it is.* The Magnificat makes us think about power—the power that we have as individuals to do extraordinary things for love and justice's sake. It makes us think about our power as a group. Do we pretend to be powerless and unconsciously allow our power to be used to oppress others, or do we stay awake to understand how our group's power is channeled for ill or for good? Mary's song is a call to stand up so that the world might be a place where all of creation can flourish—as God had intended from the very beginning.

Mary and Hagar are not the only ones staying awake at night frightened and anxious. You can no doubt name for yourself all the things that are frightening you today. We have striven so much over the past century to rise above fear and oppression, and we have created a civilization with kinder ethical norms and laws. Yet even within all of what we have accomplished, power fueled by fear and hate has always persisted. Power fueled by hate says to our collective psyche that the only power that can be trusted is one that is loud, uses physical force, closes down dialogue, requires sameness over unity, requires absolute control. Mary's song, the Magnificat, reminds us that this is not true. This is not true!

This Advent season when Mary sings "God has scattered the proud in the thoughts of their hearts," she reveals the short-term power of hate. She sings of the enduring power that can be trusted because God "sees" us and God "hears" us and chooses to become embodied as one of us in the person of Jesus.

Jesus echoes his mother's Magnificat in Luke chapter four when he says, "I am called to preach good news to the poor, to release all the prisoners, to give sight to the blind and to let the oppressed people become free."

Jesus lived each day relating to everyone and every institution with the outlook of what our power relationships *should be*—of what the divine had intended for us. Since he was a member of the most vulnerable group,

Jesus called out oppression when he saw it. Jesus wept with those who weren't healed as well as rejoiced with those who were; every time Jesus publicly blessed the validity of women, lepers, and foreigners, he was calling out the hypocrisy of his religion.

Jesus grieved that people were dying under oppression needlessly. Jesus understood how our human and spiritual fates are bound together. Those who were blinded and imprisoned by their privileged status and those literally blinded and in prison because of their poverty and class were both trapped by the unjust systems. Jesus preached, knowing his words and actions were a matter of life and death, and he did not sugarcoat or mince words.

What does it mean to live free?

Well, one way to answer that is to think of how we are captive. I think about all the checkboxes we have come to take for granted and that keep us trapped into categories whose mere existence reveals assumptions of mistrust, fear, and hate. You know the checkboxes: race, gender, sexual orientation, income level, immigrant, undocumented, religion: Muslim/Christian, Jewish, Sikh, Buddhist, Atheist.

The checkboxes trap all of us. We are all hurt by the mistrustful assumptions and seeds of fear and hate they create.

What does it mean to live free? Jesus said it best in the Gospel of John: "The truth will set you free…and the truth is this: Just as I have loved you, you also should love one another."

Today, we are experiencing for ourselves that bullying is on the rise among children and adults. Women are being sexually objectified without impunity, swastikas are being painted on churches, graffiti is popping up calling Muslims and immigrants "terrorists," and our gay children and adults are being targeted. Talks of Muslim registries and anti-Semitic rhetoric are happening at the highest level of our government. My friends, as Christians our love for one another has to include the defense of our democratic ideals.

What does it mean to live free?

It means we must acknowledge not only that we need one another to fully know God, but how we have inflicted pain; we can't just hold hands, pray together, and move on. Jesus understood then and teaches us today that accountability is part of love and freedom and that what is needed is a transfiguration of humanity—of each one of us—and we need to lean toward one another to be transfigured by God. I like the way theologian Mayra Rivera puts it:

> In Jesus' transfiguration the disciples behold both the brilliance of Jesus' glory and his relationship to those prophets who preceded him: Elijah and Moses. Just as Elijah and Moses' legacy left their mark on Jesus, our "past relations leave their marks in our bodies. The Other's face, her/his skin, indeed her/his whole body bears the marks of past encounters—signs of renewal as well as scars. These scars are never absent from our encounters. When we see, hear, or touch one another, we touch upon the Other's scars…with the hope for healing. As we emerge from honest encounters with one another, we like Jesus, can become brilliant lights of hope—we can come forth as new creatures, our scars become transfigured in the divine embrace where God is present. Again, and again, and again."[19]

The power of love that transfigures us in this divine embrace risks everything because it sees the abundant life that God desires and intends for us! It is already here. We in this church have come to experience glimpses of this power of love, and it's what makes us who we are. We have had these transfiguration moments with one another, and we will risk everything to have these over again and again! It is important, nevertheless, to be reminded that Jesus flat out tells us that this power of love will lead us into conflict and the power of hate often wins in the *short term*.

This Advent season we need to light our candles of hope, love, and peace with our eyes wide open in prayer—that is, wide open to speak out against the first sign of a distorted word against one another and an unjust law or treatment, just as we have always done. Our hope is that every time that hate triumphs in the short term, we will not be discouraged. Over human history, while hate has triumphed, it has never been able to eradicate the power of love of the resurrected Christ. It rises up in suffragettes, Sojourner Truth, Corrie Ten Boom, Dietrich Bonhoeffer,

Fannie Lou Hamer, Martin Luther King Jr., Mandela, and others whose names we don't know.

This Advent season we are called to be the hope for our communities by remembering that nobody's free until everybody's free. And because Advent is a season of waiting in hope, we must patiently consider how God is calling each one of us individually, and also as a group, to use our particular gifts and power for this urgent work.

The kingdom is not only beyond our efforts; it is even beyond our vision. We accomplish in our lifetime only a tiny fraction of the magnificent enterprise that is God's work. Nothing we do is complete, which is a way of saying that the kingdom always lies beyond us.

This is what we are about. We plant seeds that someday will grow. We water seeds already planted, knowing they hold future promise. We cannot do everything, and there is a sense of liberation in realizing that. This enables us to do something and do it very well. It may be incomplete, but it is a beginning, a step along the way, an opportunity for the Lord's grace to enter and do the rest.

We may never see the end results, but that is the difference between the master builder and the worker.

We are workers, not master builders; ministers, not messiahs.

We are prophets of a future not our own.

My friends, during this Advent season expect the angel Gabriel to visit you and whisper, "Do not be frightened!" For God *sees* and *hears* you. God is faithful. Will you join God in bearing witness? Will you sing? And like Mary, may you say "yes!"

Amen.

This Week

Make a list of the places you feel like you are called to invest your life and time. To what are you saying "yes"? To what would you like to say "yes" but it scares you a bit? How might you stand in your truth and proclaim what you know to be true?

Questions for Reflection and Discussion

1. What unique challenges faced both Nancy Hastings Sehested and Isabel Docampo in their callings?

2. Nancy said that Mary "calls her back to herself." What do you think about that? Do you identify with her statement about Mary?

3. Isabel shares her story in taking a trip to Cuba and being invited to preach and experiencing the intersection of her identities. Have you ever had a moment like that? Has anyone encouraged you to take a full look at the intersection of your identities?

4. How did the Magnificat sound coming from these two different preachers? With whom did you identify?

5. At the end of Isabel's sermon, she asked the congregation, "Will you join God in bearing witness? Will you sing?" To what are you being called to bear witness? What song are you being called to sing?

6. If you also claim Baptist identity, how do these stories help you understand what being Baptist means to you?

Endnotes

[1] Nancy Hastings Sehested, discussion with the author, October 26, 2016.

[2] Ibid.

[3] Ibid.

[4] Ibid.

[5] Ibid.

[6] Ibid.

[7] Ibid.

[8] Ibid.

[9] Ibid.

[10] Ibid.

[11] Nancy Hastings Sehested, "Hopes and Fears," sermon preached at Circle of Mercy Congregation, Asheville, North Carolina, December 21, 2014.

[12] Isabel Docampo, discussion with the author, October 26, 2016.

[13] Ibid.

[14] Ibid.

[15] Ibid.

[16] Ibid.

[17] Ibid.

[18] Ibid.

[19] Mayra Rivera, *The Touch of Transcendence: A Postcolonial Theology of God* (Louisville: Westminster John Knox Press, 2007), 139.

WEEK THREE
Joy

Our week three study continues with the stories of Rev. April Baker and Rev. Kyndra Frazier as they engage with the Magnificat and their own stories.

Rev. April Baker
Pastor, Glendale Baptist Church, Nashville, Tennessee

In 1988 April Baker helped form the student chapter of the Southern Baptist Alliance at Southeastern Baptist Theological Seminary in Wake Forest, North Carolina. As a seminary student she had become connected to the formation of the Alliance as it happened just down the road in Winston-Salem. She and other students were paying close attention to the newness of this organization within Baptist life. The Alliance presence on campus as the fundamentalists took over control of her seminary raised awareness and provided connections with faculty and folks outside of the campus with others doing the same type of dissent and proclamation.

> Mary sings not that God will do these things, but that God has done them, is doing them, even now. We could take that song and sing it and listen to it and delve into its words and lines and beauty for the entire season of Advent.
>
> —April Baker[1]

The Alliance covenant especially rang true for Baker. She sees it as "good news from top to bottom." When she was finishing her degree and looking for a place to serve, the covenant was a song of hope when every door she thought possible was slamming shut.[2] April Baker looked to the generations before her to receive encouragement and wisdom. One of her sources of inspiration was Nancy Hastings Sehested. Sehested came and preached at Southeastern in chapel while Baker was a student, and soon after that Sehested was called to pastor in Memphis.

Since seminary Baker's involvement with the Alliance of Baptists has continued. She's attended annual gatherings and most recently served two terms on the board of directors as vice president from 2012–2016. She still sees the covenant as good news: "When we say the covenant together, it makes it a living document because a body of people are speaking the words and making it living. It does something to us. It reinterprets it every time the body gathers. We leave the time together and go, living and affirming who we are."[3]

Those days after seminary proved difficult in finding a ministry position in a church. She was ordained at Second Baptist Church, Kershaw, South Carolina, and would occasionally receive invitations to "speak, not preach" at local Women's Missionary Union events or retreats. Baker said she always accepted those events because she wanted little girls to see women in the pulpit.

In 2002 Baker was called to Glendale Baptist Church in Nashville as associate pastor. After she was called, two local Baptist bodies sent over messengers to meet with the church. They were informing Glendale that they could no longer be in fellowship with them because the church had called April Baker, a woman and a lesbian. The delegation insinuated that Glendale should fire her.

The church did not fire her. In fact, two and a half years later, she was called to serve as co-pastor with Amy Mears, who was also recently called to that position from outside Glendale. When asked about why she's still Baptist, she said, "Well, why not be Baptist? Free church with opportunities and freedoms is our tradition. Being called at Glendale is evidence of that."[4]

The Magnificat has spoken to April Baker over her career about her embodied place in proclaiming this gospel message of love. "The Magnificat speaks most clearly to me about the powerful voice of someone who is not allowed to have a voice. Some of that for me is from being female and from being lesbian. I came into the calling not as the first generation of Baptist women, and so I did not have to deal with some of the issues as others, like Nancy [Hastings Sehested] and Anne [Thomas Neil] did."[5]

April Baker specifically remembers the Sunday in December when she preached her sermon "The Mystery You Behold" at Glendale. She sat on the front pew of the church between two acolytes, both girls. Mia was careful to tend to her partner, Meghan. Baker sat on the pew, with her arms around both girls, as the Magnificat was read from the pulpit. She sat there, watching as the two cared for one another, drawing a comparison between Elizabeth and Mary.

As she stepped into the pulpit that day, the image of Mia and Meghan lingered with her: "There, Mary finds open arms and a warm embrace [with Elizabeth]. She finds someone who delights in her presence and calls her a blessing—not a burden, not a disgrace, not a nobody—a blessing, even to the very one from whom she seeks refuge. Mary's song pours out of her soul; how can she keep from singing? God has considered her state and looked upon her with favor. What seemed utterly unbelievable until this very minute now flows from her heart as though it has already happened."[6]

Being called "blessed" by God and being used by God is sung gospel to April Baker: "There is the confidence of spirit that dwells within me. It's not that something will happen, but that it is happening. There is an all-of-time sense to the calling of God, and once I had a sense of my own calling to pastoral ministry and awareness of my sexual orientation and chose not to live hidden, this text gave me power."[7] She is aware that she embodies a broader sense of what a preacher is, of what proclamation is, of what God's word is when it comes from a different voice and body, especially one that has been systematically excluded from pulpits.

Her benediction to you is this: "Use your voice, and sing the song that's in your heart. When you've encountered the holy, there is something of yours to bear in the world. So do it. Do it through art, preaching, kindness, presence. Sing it."[8]

"This Mystery You Behold"

A sermon preached by Rev. April Baker at Glendale Baptist Church in Nashville, Tennessee, on December 20, 2015

The scriptures today give us more than we can possibly consider in this short time of reflection we have together. There are twists and turns to explore, juxtapositions and reversals to ponder, unlikely events and even more unlikely characters to examine. We could talk about great things coming from the most seemingly insignificant places and messiahs who hail from modest means. Bethlehem was not on the Olympic committee's list of cities to host a big event. We picture it a a scenic little town filled with serenity and wonder when we sing "O Little Town of Bethlehem." To Micah it was a place of no consequence.

Today, getting to Bethlehem is a challenge. The barriers are human-made: checkpoints and walls. There is still no room in the inn for some, depending on their religion, nationality, skin color, gender identity, the list goes on.

In Micah's prophecy the one who brings security to the land is not a mighty warrior or a great queen or a good politician; it is the one who comes and feeds the flock, gives food to the ones who are hungry, provides for the ones who are vulnerable. Peace comes not by the forceful overthrowing of whatever stands in its way. Peace comes with the security of food.

Luke gives us even more to consider. What compelled Mary to visit Elizabeth? Did such a young woman travel that distance alone? What did Elizabeth think when Mary showed up at the door? It's not like she could have sent a text to say she was on the way. Imagine Elizabeth, six months pregnant, yet beyond what was considered child-bearing age. Her husband hasn't been able to utter a word since she conceived. She likely couldn't write or read. How had they communicated through those months? Those must have been trying days for them. Now her young cousin shows up, pregnant, not married, and with a story about an angel and how her baby was conceived by a holy spirit and would rule over the house of Jacob forever.

Perhaps we will spend some time reflecting on Elizabeth greeting Mary with the words, "Blessed are you among women, and blessed is the fruit of your womb." We might wonder what washed over Mary in those moments as Elizabeth gathered her in an embrace and held her close make palpable the blessing she spoke. Surely Mary came there with some trepidation even as she sought comfort in the company of her dear cousin.

Basking in that welcome and the blessing, Mary's thoughts poured out in song. From the moment the angel visited her, thoughts and feelings, hopes, fears, and wonder had been swirling inside her. But who would listen to them? She was a young woman, not yet married, and she was pregnant. Though I'm sure there were people who had plenty of words to offer to her, one thought she had anything to say that was worth hearing.

Now blessing has replaced contempt and condemnation; an embrace has replaced scorn and derision. Empowered by acceptance and love, Mary's reticence and fear subside, and she sings.

And what a song!

God has lifted up the lowly and brought down the powerful! God looked with favor upon her, even while people around her murmured behind her back. God fills those who are hungry with good things and shows mercy to generations and generations!

She sings not that God *will* do these things, but that God *has* done them, *is* doing them, even now. We could take that song and sing it and listen to it and delve into its words and lines and beauty for the entire season of Advent. As a matter of fact, we did that three or four years ago; remember?

In the story of Mary and Elizabeth, there are twists that point to the revolutionary nature of God's presence in the world. The men take a back seat. Zechariah is silenced, and for a few moments two women come together in the country—not the capital city, mind you, but out in the sticks—and testify to what God is doing in their own lives, in the lives of each other, and in all of creation. They claim the blessings of God and let the joy that comes with those blessings pour out from them. And they proclaim the coming of a power that will transform the world. Elizabeth notes it right away: "Why should I be honored with a visit from the mother of my Lord? When I heard your greeting, the baby in my womb leapt for joy."

These two mothers-to-be get it. They know what is happening is of God—that it is miracle and that the world will never again be the same. They know that the promises of God are being fulfilled. They understand an expectant kick when one is near to holy presence. In this moment of exquisite clarity, Mary and Elizabeth know the meaning of incarnation, of bearing love into the world.

Meister Eckhart, a medieval mystic and theologian, wrote, "We are all meant to be Theotokos, mothers of God. What good is it to me," he said, "if this eternal birth of the divine Child takes place unceasingly, but does not take place within myself? And, what good is it to me if Mary is full of grace and I am not also full of grace? What good is it to me for the Creator to give birth to this child if I do not also give birth to the child in my time and my culture? This, then is the fullness of time: when the Child of God is begotten in us."

If the scriptures give us more than we can possibly consider, then Meister Eckhart ups the ante. Imagine bringing God into the world. And not only imagine it, but do it. It's hard to wrap our minds and our lives around such a thought, especially considering the world we have created.

The air is polluted with greed, and the rivers are filled with disregard for anything beyond ourselves. The earth aches in its toil to sustain us, even as we use it recklessly and pour the blood of victims of war into its soil. God's beloved people seek hope, and we build walls along our borders. God's precious children run from violence, risking their lives, seeking refuge and safety, and we blame them for the violence, declaring they may not enter "our" country.

We're making a terrible mess of God's creation, and we are called to bring God into it? We'd rather find a fig leaf behind which to hide and hope that the Holy One doesn't notice our nakedness during an evening stroll. Our song is not a song of celebration and praise. At best it is a song of lament, hoping for mercy and longing for hope. All the things we might hide behind have been stripped away, and God knows our disgrace.

Even in our fear and desperation, though, somewhere within us an old tune hums, "My life flows on in endless song, above earth's lamentations. I hear the real though far-off hymn that hails the new creation. Above the tumult and the strife, I hear the music ringing. It sounds an echo in my soul; how can I keep from singing?"

On Tuesday afternoon about sixty people gathered on the steps of the city hall downtown to hear our mayor declare that Nashville is a city of hospitality, that people seeking refuge are welcome here, and that bigotry and violence toward our Muslim citizens and neighbors has no place in our city. Our neighbors from Glendale United Methodist were there. Our friends Mark and Shana, rabbis at the temple, and new friends, both named Joshua, rabbis at the West End Synagogue, were there too. Community leaders and civic leaders and religious leaders of all kinds came together to take a stand. Amy and Deborah and I had the privilege of standing with them.

How can I keep from singing?

On Thursday, Deborah and I had the chance to attend a class on understanding Islam and hear our friend Rashed Fahkruddin talk about his faith, the peace that it demands he live, and the peace that it gives to him from his devotion to it. We were humbled by his kind words about our church, which he called by name, saying that we are good partners in the work of peace. Rashed's voice is heard frequently throughout our city as one calling for people of all faiths to learn about one another's beliefs and live with acceptance and delight in our diversity.

How can I keep from singing?

On Friday night a group of Glendalers—much of this side of the sanctuary, I believe—gathered around tables downstairs and shared a meal with some folks who might have been sleeping under a bridge or might have been rousted from a doorway and told to move on if there hadn't been a warm place and a simple cot and a hot meal for them here. It's not a solution, but it is a compassionate act in an unjust circumstance. And it makes a difference.

How can I keep from singing?

Last week, world leaders gathered in Paris and created a plan to take better care of the earth. They agreed to take measures to limit global warming and to share the burden and cost of doing so with some measures of equity. The earth might have let out the breath it had been holding and inhaled a little deeper, even if it was still a bit hesitant.

How can I keep from singing?

Somehow, even in the small part of the world I inhabit, there is evidence of incarnation. I long for it. I see it. At times I even feel it kick within me. A song starts to form deep inside, waiting to be welcomed and blessed into being.

Jan Richardson says that it is blessing that has the power to help us. Mary had heard the announcement of the angel, and though she wasn't so much asked if she was willing to bear this incarnation of love into the world as told that she would do this thing, she said, "Yes. I am the Holy One's servant. Let it be with me as you have said."

Reality sets in, and she finds herself alone in a world that is dangerous for someone like her—betrothed to someone who does not want to marry her and in a situation that will bring disgrace to her family. Alone, she flees to a place of refuge, a place of safety, a place of sanctuary. She goes to her cousin Elizabeth.

There, she finds open arms and a warm embrace. She finds someone who delights in her presence and calls her a blessing—not a burden, not a disgrace, not a nobody—a blessing, even to the very one from whom she seeks refuge.

Her song pours out of her soul—how can she keep from singing? God has considered her state and looked upon her with favor. It has been named and affirmed by a woman she loves and trusts. What seemed utterly unbelievable until this very minute now flows from her heart as though it has already happened.

> "O my friends," writes Richardson, "this is what a blessing has the power to do. The blessing that Elizabeth speaks and enacts through her words, her welcome, her gift of sanctuary:
>
> Such a blessing has the power to help us, like Mary, speak the word we most need to offer.
>
> Such a blessing gives us a glimpse of the redemption that God, in God's strange sense of time, has somehow already accomplished.
>
> Such a blessing stirs up in us the strength to participate with God in bringing about this redemption in this time, in this world.
>
> Where will we go, like Mary, to find and receive such a blessing? How will we open our heart, like Elizabeth, to offer it?"

The mystery of incarnation is not so much that Holy Presence chose to dwell among us; rather, it is how we come to know and participate in Holy Presence. When the declaration is made to us, "The Holy Spirit will come over you, and the power of the Most High will overshadow you," may our response be, "Let it be with me as the Holy One has said." When a refugee appears at our door seeking sanctuary and blessing, may we feel a leap within us, an expectant kick that jolts us to bless and to embrace.

For we do not know what the one before us bears in her body, in her spirit, in her heart that will transform the world.

This mystery was celebrated by two unlikely mothers-to-be—timid, then laughing, then singing with conviction and joy they didn't know they could articulate of a new world that God has created and is creating.

Incarnation. Love dwells among us. Holy Presence has come and is coming. God-with-us. Nothing will ever be the same again.

This mystery you behold, it is the work of God. And you are invited to participate in the incarnation of love.

Rev. Kyndra D. Frazier

Associate pastor of pastoral care and counseling at First Corinthian Baptist Church, New York City

"Why Baptist? We should start with why I'm Christian!" Kyndra Frazier said when reflecting on how she's landed amid Baptist life. When Frazier encountered the Alliance of Baptists, she was a student at Candler School of Theology at Emory University in Atlanta, Georgia. She had grown up with a strong family and a committed connection to the Church of God denomination. And while quite different from Church of God, she had been attending a church in Atlanta that integrated metaphysics, Christianity, and African traditional religion when she found herself wanting a different context of ministry.

> Mary had this relational experience with the Divine that made her transcend her own interpretations of her identity and see herself anew. My work is to continue to see myself anew so I can provide a safe place for people to land where they can see themselves anew every day.
>
> —Kyndra Frazier[9]

She knew her theology was progressive, and at times she had challenges identifying as Christian because of the oppression it has perpetrated over the course of history. During Frazier's time of discernment, at the invitation of a friend, another Candler student, she began attending Oakhurst Baptist Church in Decatur, Georgia, one of the founding churches of the Alliance of Baptists.

Frazier is a life-long learner, constantly questioning, reading, and engaging with the world around her. As she learned about the Alliance, she found a theological home—one where she affirms the covenant and finds the freedom to push against it at the same time. "A lot of what we made our commitments to," she said, "is individual freedom." Because she places value on relational experience with the Divine, these freedoms transcend dogma and legalism. The freedom of the individual is valued and affirmed. In addition to the freedom of the individual, it was one of the first places where she felt she could live into her full, created identity.

She is helping advise a task group on discernment around the current language in the covenant including binary gender references and references to imperial language surrounding the Lordship of Christ: "The commitment of the Alliance to work around racial justice, gender equality, and LGBTQ advocacy is important to me. This is wonderful for someone who thought she would never be able to participate fully as an African-American woman and identify as lesbian, as queer."[10] She was later ordained at Oakhurst Baptist Church in 2012 and went through the clergy recognition process with the Alliance of Baptists.

When growing up in Charlotte, North Carolina, Kyndra Frazier's ever-present sources of inspiration came to her especially from the strong women in her life. In the Church of God there were lots of examples of women preaching. Her great-grandmothers helped charter her family church 117 years ago. Her maternal grandmother would bring Frazier with her to Bible studies in the "homes of the saints" as one of the only children. She remembers sitting and listening to these women discuss the scripture lesson. Women would lead prayers in these homes and anoint her hands as she played the piano. These women were involved in her spiritual development for as long as she could remember.

Kyndra Frazier's mother has been her prayer partner since she was eighteen and away at school. Her mother has gone on a long journey of accepting her daughter's sexual orientation and moved to a place of accepting same-gender loving couples. "My mother's evolution," Frazier said, "exemplifies what it means to love unconditionally. So what do I need to do to embrace her and others more fully? It's a question I'm always asking."[11]

Kyndra Frazier sees her preaching as honoring these women and their presence in her life. This area of generational identity, especially, connects Frazier to the Magnificat in the Gospel of Luke. She is reminded of what she believes was Mary's faithfulness—to not be moved by external appearances—particularly when you have a divine internal revelation.

The Magnificat speaks to her when it comes to honoring her call and her identity. Frazier came out based on a conversation she had with God. She remembers begging God to take away her queerness and that God never took it away. The answer that came to her from God, she says, was, "You've always been okay, but you never asked me." She further stated, "I relied on external interpretations. This was a saving moment in my life."[12]

For Kyndra Frazier to accept her full identity and stand behind a pulpit is powerful for her. It's a gift to her and to the world to fully embrace her identity: "It's still audacious to be in someone's pulpit when people believe that you aren't supposed to be preaching. But God transcends respectability politics, legalism, and religious dogma. We can't allow people to get in the way of what God has called us to do and be in the world. That's where Mary was. It's powerful to see her transformation."[13]

Frazier ministers as the associate pastor of pastoral care and counseling at First Corinthian Baptist Church in Harlem. As she does, she works continually to be aware of her own identity so she can continue to offer safe spaces where others can engage with their identities.

Kyndra Frazier's benediction to you is this: "Mary said yes to God and to herself. It's a different thing when we say God accepts us but we don't accept ourselves. Mary gave herself a yes, and it's a celebration! So say YES to yourselves! Love yourselves!"

"To Be Young, Gifted, Queer, and Christian"

A sermon inspired by the prophet Isaiah and Mary's song in Luke, preached by Rev. Kyndra Frazier at Dream Life Fellowship Church in Decatur, Georgia

This was a time of political unrest, and the nation of Judah is believing the hype. Assyria is expanding and already attacking Israel and Syria to the north. Judah has refused to join a coalition with Israel and Syria to resist the expansion.

Consequently, Judah was attacked by Israel and Syria in retaliation. The prophet Isaiah has told the nation of Judah emphatically, "Do not make any alliances. Only trust in Jehovah; Jehovah's got you." However, King Ahaz of Judah rejects Isaiah's advice and asked Assyria to come to his aid. Assyria accepts, and all havoc has broken out. The Israelites are scared, y'all, and are trying to do all they can do to beseech the Divine's intervention through sacrifice.

Now, imagine with me you are a camera man or woman raised at a high angle to capture the nation of Judah in action. You look through your lens, and these Israelites are running frantically and desperately in and out of their place of worship. They are scared.

There's a man over there; he's thinking, "What have we done? What can I do to change this situation? What can I sacrifice?" That woman right there, she just watched her house burn to the ground. She notices that her stash of sacrificial offerings is still intact, so she grabs them and dashes immediately to the temple. Right there, we find the priest walking solemnly down the aisle toward the altar with his best garments, the sweetest smelling incense in hand, and pulling behind him a fatted calf all prepared for sacrifice; it is without blemish.

He looks to be respectable, in order, following sacrificial etiquette to a T. He is fierce in his discipline of religious practice. SUDDENLY, a bright light appears, and God's voice drops, and he calls the priest by name and says (remember, you got this all on film), "[Insert your name] Kyndra, what is wrong with you? Why are you runnin' around like this? Don't you know that I don't really need your offering? All I really want is you. It's not about these animals, really, but it is about our relational experience in this process. I mean, when you sacrifice, you give over to me what you believe I've already given to you. It's more about how we build community with each other. But you keep actin' like it's about how often you pray, how respectable your image is to other people, how much people are gonna accept you, how much you look the part that allows you to fit in and be comfortable. You have forgotten that you are the sacrifice. It is in your willingness to be uniquely and authentically you that you become the divine gift and transcend humanity. Your hiding behind religious constructs made by man and presented as what holy looks like is the hype; don't believe it. When you hide aspects of yourself I created, you dilute your anointing and my power. That's not who we agreed you would be when you came to this side. When you reject parts of yourself and attempt to conceal the things that make you the unique gift I sent to this world, you eclipse my ability to operate fully in the world. You hoard a divine light that's meant to be gifted to the world."

The light and God's voice leave as quickly as they entered in.

Your camera just captured the inception of Israel's demise because of its disobedience and sinfulness. It is important for me to lift the metaphysical definition of sin. Metaphysics is the branch of philosophy that seeks to explain the abstract, the nature of being. In *The Revealing Word*, a metaphysical dictionary, sin is error-thinking and the failure to express the attributes of this Creative Energy we call God, such as love, life, intelligence, and wisdom. Sin in this context is only redeemed through a mental process, by an inward turning and a renewal of the mind, as we see in Romans 12:2: "Be ye transformed by the renewing of your mind." Israel's sinfulness was their error-beliefs that

1. Jehovah could not deliver them,
2. Assyria would save them, and
3. That respectability politics is holiness, and holiness is based on behavior rather than embracing the uniqueness of all of who we are. Isaiah reminds us that holiness is not based on behavior or the evidence of consistent and frequent engagement in religious practice; it is the measure of our authenticity, our willingness to be vulnerable enough to stand fully in who God has called us to be. This is holy.

On Sunday, June 12, at Pulse nightclub around midnight, I imagine Edward Sotomayor, Stanley Almodovar III, Eric Rivera, Peter Gonzalez-Cruz, Kimberly Morris, Eddie Justice, and Darryl Burt, just to name a few of the victims, were engaging the practice of holiness as the dance floor yielded to their queer bodies in a place they identified as being one of freedom, where they could all be themselves, able to embrace their queer identity (and I am using queer as an umbrella term for LGBTQ), without monitoring who was around, worrying about their job being in jeopardy, or worse yet, think through if their lives would be in danger in this safe place.

It would be at 2 AM, a couple of hours later, that Omar Mateen would send persons enjoying themselves at Pulse nightclub into crisis, just as we saw in Israel.

Crisis, I believe, takes place one of two ways, either externally or internally, and at times they can happen simultaneously. Many prayers have been lifted for the victims, survivors, and their family members; however, I am unsure how many have been lifted for Omar and his family. He not only caused a crisis, but he was in crisis. I imagined that Omar believed the hype. Omar's crisis, I believe, is multilayered.

I believe it is safe to say that internal crisis generally, and particularly for Omar, comes from not knowing who we are and/or knowing who we are and living suppressed lives, subjugated by our own and other persons' judgments of us, oppressed by our own error-thinking. Omar did not know who he was and was not hospitable to himself enough to embrace all of his identities, particularly his queer identity.

Omar Mateen's murdering of forty-nine persons put me in contact with my adolescent and young adult self. The Orlando tragedy made me taste the fear and crisis I experienced prior to accepting myself as queer, lesbian, same-gender loving. I remember the summer before my freshman year in high school, being in the Love of Learning program and staying on the campus of Davidson College. There was a girl in my class, named Joy, I played basketball with. She was very touchy-feely publicly with another female classmate. Others and I used to give her an extremely hard time, often talking about her behind her back and making side comments about her being gay. My internalized homophobia attempted to murder the holiness that Joy was operating in. You see, I wanted her freedom even in the ninth grade. It got to the point where Joy had become so frustrated with our negative commentary that she one day grabbed the hand of Catherine (the girl we suspected she was with) and walked down the hallway screaming and crying, "Yeah, I'm gay, SO WHAT, SO WHAT, WHAT NOW?!"

Now, almost twenty years later myself and my friend Linda (another peer that attended the program) have come to live in holiness, accepting fully our identities as same-gender loving, as lesbian, as queer.

It is important for me to lift this narrative in my life because I believe I have not remembered enough what it is like to be uncomfortable with whom you are, the gifts you bring, and the uniqueness God has crafted you in. Not only did the Orlando shooting make me remember my own coming-out story, but it made me somewhat fearful to be out. For about a day I considered if I was putting myself at jeopardy, if I am too queer, too bold, too me.

Before I could give myself any answers, Spirit stepped in to remind me to not believe the hype and cautioned me to look at history.

You see, as a queer person it can be easy to believe the hype of our history. The 1912 Portland vice scandal refers to the discovery of a gay male subculture in the U.S. city of Portland, Oregon, following the arrest and interrogation of nineteen-year-old Benjamin Trout for shoplifting. Trout told his interrogators he had been "corrupted by a number of men in town." This prompted police investigations and led to the arrest of "dozens of men and youths for crimes ranging from so-called indecent acts of sodomy."

In 1920 Harvard University enacted secret courts to out gay professors and students, consequently expelling and firing those who were identified as gay. Beginning in 1916 a blue discharge, also known as a blue ticket, was a form of administrative military discharge that was neither honorable nor dishonorable. It was the discharge of choice for commanders seeking to remove homosexual service members from the ranks. Service members holding a blue discharge were subjected to discrimination in civilian life and denied the benefits of the GI Bill. Because of the criminalization of being queer, gay culture was pushed underground, and this is where the speakeasies in the 1920s, much like the club of contemporary times, became a safe haven for LGBTQ bodies.

It would be at 1:20 AM on June 28, 1969, at the Stonewall Inn, located in Greenwich Village, a neighborhood of Manhattan, New York City, that the gay liberation movement and modern fight for LGBTQ rights in the United States was born, known as the Stonewall riots. Gay Americans in the 1950s and 1960s faced an anti-gay legal system. There were very few establishments that welcomed openly gay people, and those that did were often bars, although bar owners and managers were rarely gay. These bars were not given liquor licenses, because they were considered to be disorderly, due to serving the "disorderly" population of queers.

At the time Stonewall Inn was owned by the Mafia and known as the gay bar in the Village, catering to the most marginalized people in the gay community, from drag queens, transgender people, effeminate young men, butch lesbians, male prostitutes, and homeless youth. Police raids on gay bars were routine in the 1960s. However, officers quickly lost control of the raid at the Stonewall Inn to a crowd who had grown weary of being oppressed, being criminalized (often thrown in jail to "clean up the city"), and being subjected to discrimination. It would be the voice of black butch lesbian Storme De Larverie, also an entertainer, who when arrested at the riot shouted to the crowd, "Why don't you guys do something?" that would trigger the Stonewall riots. Also, from 1952 to 1971 the American Psychological Association would identify homosexuality as a psychological disorder. Can you imagine, about forty-five years ago I could not have legitimately stood before you to preach this very queer sermon because you all would view me as diseased?

It is apparent in looking at history that there are those that existed and exist now who would attempt to make me believe that my queerness is anti-God, sacreligious, and an abomination. To be young, queer, gifted, and Christian; to be young, queer, gifted, and black; to be young queer, gifted, and human means to practice holiness. Not the holiness the Israelites were catering to when bringing sacrificial offerings before God, the holiness attached to behavior which is not holy at all. But to practice a holiness that celebrates God's creation of you, the holiness attached to your willingness to be vulnerable enough to accept yourself as is.

To the queer persons in the room today, the Orlando shooting was an invitation for me and you to love ourselves fiercely. This is the love of God and the love of self. For the remainder of this week and for the rest of your lives, I challenge each of us to practice holiness. Like Isaiah, I have been sent to caution you from making any alliances with anyone other than Jehovah. Do not align with respectability politics, because it will not save you. Do not align with venomous rhetoric from the pulpit that oppresses who God has called you to be, and do not align with your own false beliefs that tell you you can't live in and walk fully in your purpose while embracing all your identities.

Only align with the one who crafted you, the one who loves you, the one who sees beyond faults, the one who already deemed you as holy before you even came to this side. Remember, you are the sacrificial offering always. Your sacrifice becomes holy each and every time you choose to be authentically you. Amen.

This Week

Read the Magnificat out loud from different translations of Scripture. What does it sound like? Where are you lingering when you read it aloud? Reflect on that, and consider what God might be saying to you.

Questions for Reflection and Discussion

1. April Baker said, "The Magnificat speaks most clearly to me about the powerful voice of someone who is not allowed to have a voice." When is a time you felt like you didn't have a voice? Did you linger in that space? Speak up anyway? How does Mary's voice strengthen your own?

2. Kyndra Frazier spends time talking about the strength of the women who went before her in her family and in her church growing up. These women passed down a legacy to her. Who in your life has pointed you toward God and shared a legacy with you? To whom are you passing something down?

3. In April's sermon she mentions two girls in her congregation who care for one another, modeling the relationship between Mary and Elizabeth. What cherished friendships do you have in your life? How do they point you toward God?

4. Kyndra tells us about her connection to Mary's Magnificat in the way it empowered her to claim her full self as a revealing of God's creative power. In her sermon she talks about embracing all of our identities. What part of you do you need to dust off and spend some time with?

Endnotes

[1] April Baker, discussion with the author, October 19, 2016.

[2] Ibid.

[3] Ibid.

[4] Ibid.

[5] Baker, "The Mystery You Behold," sermon preached at Glendale Baptist Church, Nashville, Tennessee, December 20, 2015.

[6] Baker, discussion.

[7] Ibid.

[8] Ibid.

[9] Kyndra D. Frazier, discussion with the author, October 31, 2016.

[10] Ibid.

[11] Ibid.

[12] Ibid.

[13] Ibid.

WEEK FOUR
Love

Our final week of stories is from the third generation of Alliance of Baptists women with the stories of Rev. Maria Swearingen and Rev. Molly Brummett Wudel. Molly wasn't even born when the Alliance formed, and yet the echoes from the founders made their way to her.

Rev. Maria Swearingen

Senior co-pastor, Calvary Baptist Church, Washington, D.C.;
former associate university chaplain, Furman University,
Greenville, South Carolina

When I asked Maria Swearingen why she is Baptist, she replied, "I came into the world one kind of Baptist and came out another kind."

> If we don't sing this with love, then it's not the gospel song. So the enactment of a mother singing it while her child is brewing inside of her is emblematic of that.
>
> —Maria Swearingen[1]

Because of the elasticity of what it means to be Baptist, there has been space to be the fullness of herself and still be Baptist with other Baptists. "Clusters of people since the very beginning of Baptists have shared their understandings of Baptist identity. As long as those clusters exist, there continues to be space for me to be Baptist. We'll gather around these ideas and principles and go live, go sing in the world."[2] It's this understanding of the freedom of claiming Baptist identity that strikes a strong chord within Maria Swearingen.

Swearingen was raised in Texas as the daughter of a Puerto Rican mother and a white, Southern Baptist pastor father. When she was eighteen and beginning as a student at Baylor University, her understanding of Baptist identity looked very different. She says that she often looks at that tension and must live in the cognitive dissonance of knowing that both her understanding then and her understanding now get to define what it means to be Baptist.

The disruption she experienced while a student had a profound impact on her identity: "During the disruption is when you start looking at all of it. The disruption makes you look inward. Everyone needs to come out of something because disruption leads to transformation."³

At Baylor, she participated in the honors program Baylor Interdisciplinary Core (BIC), which opened new doors and windows to the way she saw the world. At times she was also feeling the disruption under the surface of exploring her sexual orientation, but looking further into that did not feel safe at the time. She was working to make sense of herself and her orientation. Inquisitive questions abounded during her college years.

From Baylor, Swearingen attended Duke Divinity School and graduated in 2010. Her first encounter with the Alliance of Baptists was in 2013 while a member at First Baptist Church, Greenville, South Carolina. She was invited to be on the planning team for the Alliance's annual gathering that year. Maria worked within a divinity school internship at FBC Greenville, where she also met her wife. She was also ordained by the church in November 2015.

In 2013 the gathering was planned to be in Atlanta but was relocated to Greenville due to a scheduling conflict. The relocation held a deeper meaning, though, to both the Alliance and FBC Greenville. The 2005 gathering had to be relocated from FBC Greenville because of the Alliance's stance on being welcoming and affirming to the LGBTQ community. At that time a few members of FBC Greenville had some discomfort with the possibility of a lesbian preaching during that gathering.

The return to FBC Greenville in 2013 was pregnant with meaning. Swearingen remembers looking around the room during worship at the gathering in 2013 and seeing some of those who had been previously uninvited now behind the pulpit. No one said anything about the presence of those previously excluded, but it's like everyone exhaled, she said. FBC Greenville came out in support of same-sex marriage in 2015. That was her introduction to the Alliance of Baptists, and since then she has participated enthusiastically.

She chaired the thirtieth anniversary annual gathering, which took place in Raleigh, North Carolina, in April 2017, and the church where she now pastors alongside her wife, Rev. Sally Sarratt, hosted the 2019 annual gathering. She has noted that "the Alliance is aware of its limits—

it's predominantly white—but they are not blind about it. The Alliance is honest about what's aspirational and where they are not perfect and then articulates whom they hope to be."[4]

She thinks there's even a great connection between Mary, the Magnificat, and Baptists: "Here's the handmaiden, a servant, a regular old somebody becoming a priest. It's a very Baptist notion."[5]

Her work as assistant university chaplain at Furman University was a laboratory for conversations on identity. Each Sunday when she stood before students, she was aware of the pain, questions, and joy that surrounded them. It was with that awareness that she preached two homilies, both at Advent Moravian Love feasts in 2013 and 2015 on the Magnificat. In her sermon, "God, the Caroler," from 2015, Swearingen preached,

> This is no accident. This is the genius of Luke's Gospel. This is the genius of Scripture as a whole.... It sings us away from violence and toward peace. It sings us out of brokenness and into right relationship with God and others. It sings us away from power and greed and empire and toward mutuality and forgiveness and wholeness.[6]

Maria Swearingen reflects that when singing the Magnificat, Mary feels invited to claim her identity. She uses it as her moment. Her story is transcribed on the larger story, which is a powerful invitation for everyone. "What does it mean for my embodied reality to take on and claim a portion of the text, a kind of identifying and lived incarnate reality?" Swearingen pondered. For her, Mary becomes dynamic expression of just that. She takes something older and deeper and wider than her and says this is about her and goes far beyond her at the same time. It is the deeply embodied and the deeply cosmic that can only come from God.

For Maria Swearingen, as a queer woman, Mary's Magnificat and her embodied singing remind her that at the time, Mary's body was also problematized sexually. Mary had been impregnated before marriage, and she was no longer deemed acceptable in her society. Her body was the last one that would have been accepted as the one to sing a song such as this.

Swearingen sees Mary's singing as the good news: "She's been problematized, and she's receiving this great gift, and her body is the one singing out this great dismantling gospel to the world and for all time. For me to imagine my own body that's been problematized and questioned as a body that gets to sing the Magnificat or my own version—that's an ancient gift, and I get to sing it back out to the world. That's a big deal."[7] And the Magnificat is calling the world to disruption that leads to a new identity—the upturning, uprooting challenge found in the Magnificat is Jesus's love song to the world, she says.

The awareness of the embodied aspects of preaching strikes her frequently. When she was preaching at Myers Park Baptist Church in Charlotte, North Carolina, in 2016, she felt the seriousness and sacredness in the few seconds it took her to climb the stairs up into the grand pulpit there. She felt more connected to all those who had gone before her and paved the way for her in that sensory moment.

She works to encourage young women who are called to ministry. She once met with a young queer Baptist student who was discerning her call to ministry. In that moment she was reminded that it's a very thin place where possibility and opportunity meet for many people.

Maria Swearingen's benediction to you follows: "Disruption comes when you claim embodiment. As people problematize whom you are based on your presence, keep singing. There is an ancient song that keeps showing up, and you get to claim it."[8]

"God, the Caroler"

A sermon preached by Rev. Maria Swearingen at Daniel Chapel, Furman University's Moravian Love Feast, December 6, 2015

Normally, I'm no King James reader. Mainly, it's because I feel like at any moment I might break into Hamlet's dramatic soliloquy about mortality instead of Jesus's Sermon on the Mount. It can be a bit arcane, with its "tis"es and "thou"s and "thine"s.

But sometimes the "tis"es and "thou"s and "thine"s make for incredible poetry. I mean, that was the point of this early English translation anyway—to make poetry out of an ancient manuscript, to give Hebrew and Latin and Greek a new dramatic voice. As ancient as it might seem to us sometimes, it really does sing.

Consider the prophetic voice of Zephaniah—I know, that book in the Bible I read all the time too. In Zephaniah 3:17 we hear the prophet say that "the Lord thy God is in the midst of thee, rest in His Love, He will joy over thee with singing."

Joy over thee. I don't know about you, but grammatical configurations don't lead me to use joy as a verb. I might be joyful, I might have joy, but I don't think of myself as joying. There is something captivating about joy being an action and, all the more captivating, the image of God joying over us with loud, exuberant singing.

Can you imagine God in one of those Dickens outfits—top hat, gold buttons, bells in hand—caroling up and down the street, blasting "Deck the Halls" from door to door? Goodness knows that when fire rains down and the earth quakes, no one pictures God in a caroling outfit. But if God had anything to do with getting us the stories we find in Scripture, I think it's safe to say that God's been doing a whole lot of singing for a very long time.

The writer of Luke's Gospel recounts Jesus's birth in a way that you might not notice at first glance because it sits flat on the page, no treble clefs in sight. The story is actually told in song. In fact, Jesus's birth narrative contains three, if not more, songs or hymns. You heard them read to you this evening. Mary's song, traditionally known as "the Magnificat," is sung when Mary, after being greeted by her relative Elizabeth, gives glory to God for finding favor with her, a humble servant. Zechariah's song, often referred to as "the Benedictus," takes place right after John the Baptist is born and his father, earlier silenced by the angel Gabriel, breaks forth in song. A few paragraphs later in the story, as Jesus is born in Bethlehem, the angels sing "Gloria in Excelsis" while a group of shepherds listen in wonder.

The writer of Luke tells us about Jesus's birth, not merely with words but with lyrics. These songs likely existed long before Jesus was born. Portions of them may have existed in the Jewish tradition for quite some time. Without forcing a cultural stretch here, these might have been Jesus's carols growing up. Songs of joy and remembrance. Songs that reminded people of God's presence and provision. Songs that told the story of God's work of liberation in the world. And the Gospel writer knew that he could sing the good news better than he could ever merely write it. There is something about words having rhythm and movement that makes them come alive.

And while it might feel like everything at Christmas is packaged, sealed, and stamped with a red bow for sale, including, I kid you not, a nativity set made out of chocolate, the songs are free to anyone. You know all too well that they are the heart and soul of the season. They can be sung by rich or poor, Occupy Wall Streeter or Tea Partier, extrovert or introvert, bedridden or healthy, American or Armenian.

Does every carol offer us the spirit of Christmas? Well, I suppose "Have a Holly Jolly Christmas" does make me smile, but when the final verse of "O Holy Night," written as an abolitionist anthem, comes streaming through a tenor voice—"Truly he taught us to love one another. His law is love, and his gospel is peace. Chains he shall break, for the slave is our brother. And in his name all oppression shall cease"—I am left dead in my tracks. I am repentant. I am lost and then found. I am exuberant. I am brought to life again. And slowly but surely, God's vision for humanity captures my weary imagination once again.

This is no accident. This is the genius of Luke's Gospel. This is the genius of Scripture as a whole—Greek, King James, or whatever iteration you hold dear. It sings us—it joys us—into lives of justice and mercy and self-giving, world-altering love.

It sings us away from violence and toward peace. It sings us out of brokenness and into right relationship with God and others. It sings us away from power and greed and empire and toward mutuality and forgiveness and wholeness.

You might not have much in you this holiday. Maybe this season just reminds you all the more of the ones you have lost in the past. Maybe you are struggling to pay for your Furman education or you don't know what the next stop in the road of life is for you, and happy people singing happy songs just reminds you of how happy you are not.

But listen to these songs. Consider their context.

A young woman, pregnant and terrified, is reminded by a relative that while the world might see her situation as a problem, God is forming within her very being a new Son and a new song for all of creation.

An elderly priest, left mute, silenced, and uncertain, watches his barren wife give birth to a child, and unable to even utter his new son's name, all of a sudden, his mouth is opened, and like a scroll unrolling from his tongue, he speaks a prophecy to his friends and neighbors.

A group of shepherds, certainly not white-collar in status, trying to stay awake on I-85 to make that last shipment for the night—i.e., keeping watching over their flocks by night—watch the sky light up in celestial glory as they teeter between horror and awe.

It's not all happy, friends. It's scary and vulnerable and uncertain.

But just because the thought of dressing up in that silly Dickens outfit and caroling door-to-door isn't your cup of tea does not mean you aren't a significant part of this season's chorus. All the more reason you must sing.

Because the day the music dies, you die. The day we stop singing of God's inbreaking into our realities is the day we can no longer see the world like God sees it, smell the world like God smells it, love the world like God loves it. Because when God loves something, God can't help but "joy over it with singing."

If your throat is scratchy, if your nose is clogged, if all you can do is whisper or hum the tune, for goodness' sake, do it. Let Christmas be your song. Let the message that the God of all creation, the one who pulled gems out of the depths of the sea and flung them into the night sky, the one whose voice cried "Let there be" and from this divine imagination came the aardvark and the whale and the helpless infant—let that message be your Christmas carol.

Let the message that this God was most like God in being most like us—and that we know love when we see the one who could make mountains crumble tuck himself inside the breast of his own mother.

Let that message be your Christmas carol.

Sing this season into reality. *Joy* with all you've got. Don't fake it with holiday pleasantries. You don't have the energy for that. Don't consume it with more gadgets and bows. You don't have the money for that.

Just sing it. Joy it. Carol your way to the gospel. Let God, the greatest storyteller, who sang this universe into being, sing you into being.

If you're not there yet, don't hurt yourself. See, that is what Advent is all about. Waiting. Waiting for God to meet you. Waiting for God's song to grow, like a baby, within your body and spirit.

If you can't sing it right now, let God sing it to you. Truth is, that's where the magic is anyway—when the baby-redeemer puts on that Dickens outfit and carols up and down the streets of your heart, ringing the bells of your broken spirit, *joying* over you with singing, caroling over all of creation—no matter how war-torn, how poverty-stricken, how consumer-driven, or how power-hungry it is.

And when God does this for us, we can do this for one another. Amidst so many stories of violence and brutality these last months, I don't know about you, but I've struggled for air. I've struggled to trust the thread of humanity that binds us together; I've struggled to hear the song, much less sing it.

Then I heard this story. As Greenville County seems hell-bent on refusing Syrian refugees, I read the Calgary mayor Naheed Nenshi, the first Muslim to lead a Canadian city, recount an open forum focused on the city's decision to welcome thousands of refugees. He says,

> I was a little bit nervous walking in because it was an open invitation; anybody could come, and I thought there might be some angry people or people with a lot of very difficult questions. At one point a First Nation woman stood up. I thought she was going to say, "Why are we having all this focus on these refugees when we have so many problems closer to home?" What she actually said was, "I need some help. Because I need to understand how and when they're coming. I want to make sure, and many of my First Nations colleagues want to make sure, that when these people come, we have an opportunity to have the elders there to drum them in and to do a smudge ceremony so we can welcome them to this land." [Nenshi finishes,] I might have lost it at that point.

Who are we drumming in? Who is God drumming in? Who are we joying over with singing? The Gospel calls us from the depths of who we are to ask those questions. And the answer—the wild, holy, terrifying answer—is, and always has been, every single one of us.

The writer of Luke was no dunce. How could anyone tell a story like this one without singing it? How could anyone imagine God as a baby and not turn it into a holy lullaby?

How could God not be a caroler, singing us—singing it all—back to life? Let God put on that silly outfit for you. And at least for one round, just hop in God's chorus and sing along. Amen.

"Great with Child"

A sermon preached by Rev. Maria Swearingen at Daniel Chapel, Furman University's Moravian Love Feast, December 8, 2013

Our Scripture lessons this evening bring us alongside a young woman named Mary (perhaps you've heard of her), who without any warning, planning, or intention finds herself carrying, well, God.

> The body is like Mary, and each of us has a Jesus inside. Who is not in labor, holy labor? Every creature is.
>
> —Rumi

Kicking and churning and swimming inside Mary's belly is a storyteller and a prophet and a dreamer and a lover who will love so deeply and fully that even death will not bury his love. But before we can tell any stories about Jesus, before we can see him break bread and heal wounds and tell us about a kingdom where the lion lays down with the lamb, we must see Mary, dazed by an angel's shocking news, saying with breathtaking simplicity, "Here am I."

This evening, I wonder if we can pause a moment in the midst of the storyline to imagine Mary in the unwritten moments, seconds after the angel Gabriel vanishes, or along the dirt path as she journeys from Nazareth to visit her equally shocked cousin Elizabeth, or right before she bursts forth in song about this new kingdom on its way. What about the moments between those moments? Can you see her there too? I imagine Mary catching her breath, catching her anxiety and uncertainty, sitting in stillness and solitude, hands pressed against her belly, waiting for a kick, waiting for a sound, waiting for a birth that she never saw coming.

Mary was great with child.

And within her very being, bound to her by blood and water and daily growing love, Mary was carrying God. And in carrying God, Mary was carrying all that our imaginations can bear. Mary was carrying the hope of the world, the peace of nations, the love of all peoples.

She was carrying God. She was carrying a baby. She was carrying all that there is to carry.

I suppose, though, that we could gaze upon Mary, great with child, and leave ourselves outside of the picture. I suppose we could hold this moment at arm's length and consider its abstract meaning without entering inside of it more deeply.

But the stories in Scripture are not meant for analysis or detachment. They are meant to captivate our imaginations and revive our visions. So maybe this evening we can place ourselves in Mary's shoes or sandals or even bare feet. Maybe for a few moments while we are gathered here, we can imagine our own pregnancies—perhaps for some of us, that's literal. But for many of us, we may need to press beyond the literal and imagine our souls as a womb, giving life and energy and love to whatever is growing inside of us.

But this means we must imagine God and God's vision for the world not as a concept hovering over us, but instead as a baby growing toes and fingers and spinal columns, connected to us, vulnerable to us.

Perhaps Mary is not the only one doing the carrying around here.

You may have noticed at the very top left-hand corner of your bulletin, in red print, a line from the poet Rumi. In one poem he writes, "The body is like Mary, and each of us has a Jesus inside. Who is not in labor, holy labor? Every creature is."

Rumi, a Muslim scholar and mystic, spent much of his life discovering and reimagining the dimensions of the Divine Presence. He penned these words around thirteen centuries after the birth of Jesus. I can imagine him pouring over the stories and images in the Gospels of Matthew and Luke and, with reverence and awe, connecting all of humanity to the unseen, untold moments in between the words on the page. I imagine him imagining Mary, hands pressed against her belly, waiting, listening, wondering as this unknown being takes root, takes hold, and grows within her.

"The body is like Mary, and each of us has a Jesus inside. Who is not in labor, holy labor? Every creature is."

Even you. Even me? All of us? Are we all in holy labor, carrying within our very beings the presence of the Divine?

Like Mary, we are carrying Jesus; we are carrying the Divine. We are carrying the hopes and dreams and visions that call us to love God and the world more fully.

If you could imagine yourself hands pressed against your own belly—waiting, listening, wondering—what do you hear? What do you feel? What is kicking around the walls of your soul's womb?

What are you great with this Advent season? What is growing inside of you? What is taking root and coming to life and waiting to be born?

Who is growing within you? Who is taking root and coming to life and waiting to be born?

How strange to think of God growing inside of us. How disquieting and peculiar and dismantling to imagine God as a baby. Goodness knows any linear, logical, systematic theology we've held on to for security seems to crumble before our eyes when we imagine the God of the universe, God who is mighty and all-powerful and all-knowing.

Inside our wombs, waiting to be born. How risky and messy and confusing.

Followers in the Franciscan tradition have long held that the birth of Jesus (the fancy word for this is *incarnation*, literally, God taking on human flesh) is more important than Easter itself. Without knowing God as a child growing in Mary's womb—as a baby, in need of our care and support—it is difficult to know God any other way. Even if the only way we want to imagine God is as great conqueror over death and sin, we must begin long before victory and start with vulnerability.

There are lots of reasons we may think we cannot, or we should not, carry God this way—why we think we cannot carry our dreams and visions, our courage and our love this way.

Maybe we just think it best not to imagine God this way. God is better left in the sky, lording over us, commanding and judging and tossing a few lightning bolts our way. Maybe the very thought that God is deeply bound to us and with us just feels a bit too risky.

Maybe we don't see ourselves as strong enough or worthy enough to carry God this way. Maybe we think that it's too risky, too vulnerable and susceptible to forces beyond our control. How can God, how can our visions of peace, really flourish inside our wombs? What if they don't survive? What if our souls are barren?

So we take our hands off our bellies, too terrified to imagine anymore, too tired to believe that anything is really growing at all, too traumatized by wounds from the past to believe that we are capable of loving whatever or whomever is being birthed within us.

Sometimes life doesn't feel very pregnant with possibility or hope or peace or joy and certainly not love. Sometimes life feels barren, empty, dreamless, violent, disordered, and destructive.

Sometimes when we press our hands against our soul's womb, we feel great with nothing but fear and doubt and self-hatred and despair in the face of the world's needs, of our own needs.

And yet God comes to us not as a mighty wizard, obliterating all the things that inhibit us or wound us or exhaust us or embitter us.

God comes to us in the womb, needing us, desiring us, growing inside of us. And then as we wait and, slowly but surely, as our dreams and visions and desires and our own divine nature grows within us, we find ourselves in labor, holy labor, giving birth to God. We find ourselves feeding and clothing and loving the One who has made all things new.

Maybe this is why Jesus tells his disciples that the way he will really know who is following him, the way he will really know who is in it for love, are those who feed and clothe and visit their neighbors in need. Maybe he remembered stories of an early manger and two wide-eyed parents, and he couldn't help but say according to Matthew 25, "For I was hungry, and you gave me something to eat; I was thirsty, and you gave me something to drink; I was a stranger, and you invited me in; I needed clothes, and you clothed me; I was sick, and you looked after me; I was in prison, and you came to visit me."

I was a baby, and you held me.

Maybe we've all got a better shot at loving the world with gladness, loving our neighbor as ourselves, loving God with all our hearts and all our minds and all our souls when God is born in us and has time and space to grow within us as nothing more and nothing less than a baby. And maybe that kind of God can establish love where we least expect it.

What is Advent, anyway? Best I have gathered, it's the preparation of Christ's entry into the world. But if the story of Mary tells us anything, the coming of Christ isn't high in the sky stuff. It's deeply bound to our bodies and spirits and very lives. It involves us. We are a part of Christ's coming, because we are all Mary, hands held against our bellies, pregnant with the Divine presence, waiting, listening, growing.

And, like us, the whole world is pregnant with expectation.

O holy Child of Bethlehem, descend to us, we pray; cast out our sin, and enter in; be born in us today.

Be born in us today.

O God, wherever we may be, whether ready or wary,

we are great with something.
Give us the courage, the grace, the love
to be great with you. Amen.

Rev. Molly Brummett Wudel

Co-pastor, Emmaus Way, Durham, North Carolina

Molly Brummett Wudel has always known part of her identity was the woman she was named after: "It's strange growing up with parents who named me after Rev. Dr. Molly T. Marshall. This notion of being Baptist, being named after this significant Baptist theologian, means that I was named to not be afraid to stand up to the powers that be."[10] She said her parents always told her, "Whatever you do professionally, we named you after her because she understands the good news of the gospel."

> We are called and invited to dance and be about this good news. —the place where the world has been made whole in such a way by Mary's song. It disrupts all of it and shakes us up. I need it.
>
> —Molly Brummett Wudel[9]

Molly T. Marshall was one of the professors at Southern Baptist Theological Seminary in Louisville, Kentucky, who was systematically removed by fundamentalists on the board of trustees. A PBS documentary was even created about her story and journey, *Battle for Their Minds*.[11] She now serves as the president at Central Baptist Theological Seminary in Shawnee, Kansas. Living into the work of her namesake, Molly Brummett Wudel—born two years after the formation of the Alliance of Baptists—has always understood that being Baptist meant freedom.

Growing up in Tennessee as a white Baptist female, she always knew about the Alliance, as individuals in her home church supported the organization. But her entry point did not come until she attended divinity school at Wake Forest School of Divinity in Winston-Salem, North Carolina.

While in school Molly Brummett Wudel met Chris Copeland, who had previously been on staff as one of the co-directors of the Alliance. As she wrestled with whether to be ordained Baptist, she remembers a conversation she had with Chris. He advised her, "Molly, you are a trailblazer. It's in your DNA and how you're wired. You're about justice and radical inclusion. The Alliance is a trailblazing group of Baptists. Those are your people."

That sounded like good news to Brummett Wudel, and so did the Alliance covenant: "The attention to the proclamation of the good news and justice is the heart of who we are. I'm tired of apologizing and assumptions being made of what it means to be a Christian and to be Baptist. This covenant is the heart of it. It points to the radical love of God—open, expansive—and I'm not ashamed of that."[12] She was later ordained in 2013 at First Baptist Church, Jefferson City, Tennessee, and called to an Alliance congregational partner, Knollwood Baptist Church, Winston-Salem, North Carolina, as associate pastor.

Brummett Wudel currently serves as co-pastor at Emmaus Way Church in Durham, North Carolina, which as a congregation does not identify with any denomination. Even though not serving in a Baptist church, she says Emmaus Way very clearly knows they called a female Baptist pastor. She continues in her Baptist tradition, even though questioning it as she goes, and loves to sing the truth that Baptists came from the radical reformation. Being Baptist means standing on edges and bringing about justice in society—there's no hierarchy informing us what to do, and that is part of the beauty of being Baptist, she says.

This is part of what connects her to the Magnificat and to Mary. She is fascinated by Mary: "This idea of agency, of co-creation with God and living into this idea of 'yes' is good news to me. What would it look like if we read this as instead of God telling Mary what to do, that Mary is hearing a call and willingly choosing to say yes? How does that invite us into that call of revolution?[13]"

The Magnificat has shaped Molly in her ministry. It gives her the freedom to fully embrace who she is and the call as Christians to be about love and light in the world. She believes the Magnificat is a call to change the world: "If Mary could do it and go against so many societal judgments and structures, if she was brave enough to enter in and say yes, then I can too."[14] Molly has said yes in various ways throughout her ministry, like choosing to preach.

Molly Brummett Wudel's sermon on the Magnificat was preached in 2012 at Green Street United Methodist Church, the site of Molly's internship placement during divinity school. It was during a summer sermon series on calling. In this sermon, "Mary: A Call to Revolution," Molly Brummett Wudel proclaimed,

> A revolution is a radical and pervasive change in society and the social structure, a marked change in something, a single turn of its kind. The Magnificat marked such a change. This song of Mary is more than a beautiful anthem we proclaim at Christmas. It is a revolutionary, prophetic song that gives voice to the call of God for her life and for ours.[15]

Brummett Wudel's revisits the revolution Mary sparked with the Magnificat almost daily. She believes that Mary sings a constant invitation to engage in the revolution of the kingdom some way, every day. Mary is as much a part of her as anyone, as a reminder and nudging of how she is called to bear God in the world, daily.

Molly Brummett Wudel's benediction to you is that "we would willingly and boldly embrace the revolution of the Magnificat and dance in that truth in our whole beings, in the world, and in our churches. We would embody the Magnificat in all we do."[16]

"Mary: A Call to Revolution"

A sermon preached by Rev. Molly Brummett Wudel at Green Street United Methodist Church in Durham, North Carolina, on July 15, 2012

This summer, we are tracing the theme of call and vocation. Besides Esther, we've spent most of the summer looking at men and their call. For the record, I love men. I am not a male-hater (most days). But as a female who is called, I could not let the opportunity pass to not focus on a woman's call story this morning. We have so much to learn from women called by God. For far too long in our history, women remain an afterthought instead of a forethought.

Today, Mary, shall no longer be an afterthought. A confession before I begin, though: Mary hardly played a role in my Christian upbringing. Perhaps this sermon is an attempt to reclaim her absence in my faith formation.

Growing up, I knew Mary was the mother of Jesus. I always desired to be her in a Christmas pageant. That was the extent of Mary for me. I sadly think that is the case for many Protestants. Back in the day, many church fathers got agitated with exalted language that made Mary a co-redeemer of humanity, and so the instutitional church, in turn, become afraid to talk of her call. We honor Mary as the mother of Jesus, God incarnate, but we Protestants rarely look to her example.

Despite this truth, one could easily argue that no woman has influenced Western history and culture more than Mary. With hope and joy we should enter her call story, rely on it, lean into it, and allow it to find root within our Protestant selves. So, today, this Baptist working for the Methodists while trying to channel my Catholic brothers and sisters will attempt to bring some clarity, insight, or maybe just a few ramblings to Mary, the mother of God, and her call to revolution.

This passage bears the question, "Is this call really meeting Mary at her point of deepest gladness?" For in today's call story in Luke 1, we have an unwed girl told by the angel Gabriel, "You will conceive in your womb and bear a son, and you will name him Jesus. He will be great and will be called the Son of the Most High, and the Lord God will give to him the throne of his ancestor David. He will reign over the house of Jacob forever, and of his kingdom there will be no end."

She is only thirteen—fifteen tops. Her moments of deep gladness should consist of hanging out with her girlfriends by the well or spending time with Joseph as they prepare for their wedding. But a pregnancy? A deep gladness?

"How can this be?"

She hesitates and questions her call just like Moses, Jeremiah, Isaiah, Peter, and countless others before and after her questioned theirs. She wanted to know exactly whose idea it was and exactly how it would happen. She wanted to make sense out of what made no sense—that God chose her to bear God incarnate. She takes one elongated pause and audibly gives voice to a single question: "How can this be, Gabriel?"

"How in the *world* can I, an unwed, lowly peasant girl be bringing in God incarnate?"

"How can this be?" That is all she asked.

Unlike Moses, who was called, who questioned, and who took multiple pauses and made multiple objections, Mary only took one pause. One moment. If I were Mary, I would have been like Moses.

There are several questions I would have raised: Will Joseph stick around? Will my parents still love me? Will my friends stand by me? Will the pregnancy go all right? Will the labor be hard? Will there be someone to help me when my time comes? Will I know what to do? You say that the child will be the king of Israel, but what about me? Will I survive his birth? What about me?

But Mary doesn't ask all those questions. She doesn't behave like Moses. She leans into it. She trusts. She answers the call. Mary had every reason to run screaming from this angel, every cause to consider him an angel of darkness.

For having a child out of wedlock, she could be stoned for adultery. She could spend the rest of her days in even deeper poverty, struggling to keep herself and her child fed. But she doesn't reject God's ridiculous plan to inhabit her womb.

If I were Mary, I'd feel that this call was not my deepest gladness but my greatest burden. I would have kicked and screamed and told God she picked the wrong person for this job. No thank you. No way am I bearing a child before I have to! Yet, despite reservation, Mary proclaimed in Luke, "Here am I, the servant of the Lord; let it be with me according to your word."

Mary entered into a call not of her own choosing, yet Mary did not shrink from the call. She instead enriched all humanity by her willing participation. Mary willingly chose to enter into the call, enter into the revolution, enter into the position to help meet the needs of the world. All of creation held its breath, hoping Mary would answer the call. And she did.

She gratefully participated in a part of the story that everyone was waiting for. Mary is not overwhelmed by God's call but lets it flow through her in song of joy for God's justice. She sings a song that captures her moving response to God's call. Mary had nine months to make sense of her call and what it all meant. Yet it did not take her nine months to make sense of it all.

No, Mary's soul "magnified the Lord" moments after hearing and accepting the call. This peasant girl, who knew the morning sickness, the swollen body, and the labor pains were coming, sang praises to God and of God.

In the Magnificat, beginning in Luke 1:46, she proclaims:

> My soul glorifies the Lord and my spirit rejoices in God my Savior,
>
> for he has been mindful of the humble state of his servant.
>
> From now on all generations will call me blessed, for the Mighty One has done great things for me—holy is his name.
>
> His mercy extends to those who fear him, from generation to generation.
>
> He has performed mighty deeds with his arm; he has scattered those who are proud in their inmost thoughts.
>
> He has brought down rulers from their thrones but has lifted up the humble.
>
> He has filled the hungry with good things but has sent the rich away empty.
>
> He has helped his servant Israel, remembering to be merciful to Abraham and his descendants forever, even as he said to our fathers.

I wonder what her society thought when people heard these words? A revolution is a radical and pervasive change in society and the social structure, a marked change in something, a single turn of its kind. The Magnificat marked such a change.

This song of Mary is more than a beautiful anthem we proclaim at Christmas. It is a revolutionary, prophetic song that gives voice to the call of God for her life and for ours. Was it for them what it was for some of us the first time we heard the Beatles' auspicious "Revolution"?

You say you want a revolution, well, you know, we all want to change the world. You tell me that it's evolution, well, you know, we all want to change the world.[17]

Did the Magnificat ignite the revolution and passion then that the sixties did for our society? Did the Magnificat begin a transformation of all people like sixty-eight and sixty-nine began in America? In the Magnificat, the incarnation of God that Mary announced meant the inversion of conventional wisdom. Dethroning political power, plundering the rich, and redistributing food supplies signaled a new age and order. God changes the values of life.

Her song indicates the greatest revolution this world has ever and will ever know. Mary's song proclaims, "You say you want a revolution, well, you know, it's already here."

The Magnificat demonstrates that Mary was a prophet called by God. She heard the voice of God, listened to the call, and spoke to the ways in which God entered into the broken world. We stand closer to Mary's call than we might want to believe. We exist closer to her response than we might want to imagine. If we identify a prophetic call as hearing the voice of God, discerning that all is not right with the world, and doing something about it, then we, too, are called to be the prophets of our day and age.

Theologian Cynthia Rigby writes that Mary "reveals what it means for us…to bear God to the world. What it means for us to enter into the revolution. What does it mean to say that Mary— and we—are the bearers of God? It might have been tempting for Mary, and it might be for us, to exempt ourselves from the mission to which we are called. 'Sorry, Gabriel,' we might say, 'I'd like to…but it's simply not within my power.' So often we miss out on participating in the grace-full work of God because—unlike Mary—we refuse to acknowledge its impossibility. Instead, we work to make it manageable."[18]

Incarnation is not about manageability.

If we are to be the prophets that God calls us to be, then we must hear Gabriel saying, "Nothing will be impossible with God," nod our heads up and down with Mary, and say with her, "Here am I, the servant of the Lord."

We, by Mary's example, must continue to sing and to live the Magnificat into this day and age.

We, like Mary, are called to be risk-takers, poets, philosophers, creative agents in God's creativity rather than passive vessels and bystanders. Protestants often dismiss Mary as a passive vessel that bore God rather than the active agent of justice ushering in a revolution. Mary is easier to deal with when she is a flat character rather than the dynamic presence bearing God. Mary's call forces us to realize we must trust God even when we can't track God.

We, like Mary, must sing a song of revolution and dance.

We, like Mary, are called to bear God even when it is socially unacceptable. We are called to bear God in situations that are not always easy, comfortable, or ideal. We are called to face the morning sickness, swollen bodies, and labor pains in order to bring in great compassion, love, and hope to places of great sorrow and sadness. We are called to be swollen with compassion like Desmond Tutu speaking out against the injustice of apartheid. Like Mother Teresa taking the last pair of shoes, even though too small, so others could walk comfortably. Like Ezell Blair, Franklin McCain, Joseph McNeil, and David Richmond sitting down at Woolworth's in Greensboro for civil rights. And like Rabbi Josh being one prophetic voice, among many, against Amendment One.

It is not too late to hear the call.

It is not too late for your greatest gladness found in the revolution of incarnation and the world's greatest need to meet; it is not too late to respond to the call to bear God into this world.

We, like Mary, are called to be storytellers of the revolution. We must tell the world of the radical revolution the incarnation brings. We must show the world how love came down, how it keeps coming down, how with Mary we behold it, and how with Mary we join together and say, "Here we are, willing to bear God into this world and to dance the dance of revolution. Your servants are ready, Lord." Amen.

"Hope"

A sermon preached by Rev. Molly Brummett Wudel at Emmaus Way in Durham, North Carolina on December 4, 2017

I don't know about you, but hope is hard for me these days. If I'm being completely honest, hope has been hard for me for a while now. Now I'm not talking about the temporary hope we have when we want this thing or that action to happen. I'm talking about the hope that comes with deep belief in the inbreaking kingdom of God—in knowing God is at work in the world and in our own lives in such a way that it matters—that the way things are not the way things will always be.

Just look around—look at our world, our country, our city, the harsh realities of too many folks' lives, even some of ours. Hope is hard to grasp in times such as these.

And yet we are invited to hope this time every year. Hope. Damn hope that won't let us get off the hook even when we fiercely want it to.

Pauli Murray speaks of hope this way in her poem "Dark Testament":

Hope is a crushed stalk
Between clenched fingers.
Hope is a bird's wing
Broken by a stone.
Hope is a word in a tuneless ditty —
A word whispered with the wind,
A dream of forty acres and a mule,
A cabin of one's own and a moment to rest,
A name and place for one's children
And children's children at last...
Hope is a song in a weary throat.

Give me a song of hope
And a world where I can sing it.
Give me a song of faith
And a people to believe in it.
Give me a song of kindliness
And a country where I can live it.
Give me a song of hope and love
And a brown girl's heart to hear it.[19]

Mary had hope. We saw that last week as we began to look at Mary as active agent of justice ushering in a revolution—the revolution of Jesus the Christ, first and foremost—through the singing of the Magnificat. And we named last week, and it's worth repeating that Mary is easier to deal with when she is a flat character rather than the dynamic presence bearing God. For when she is flat, she doesn't really have hope. But flat she is not, and bearing God she did, for hope she clinged to.

She held on to hope as she sang a song of revolution that embodies the hope-iest of hopes. In the Magnificat, Mary proclaims that God extends, performs, scatters, brings down, lifts up, fills, sends away, helps. And God is so not helping out those in power, so much so that the Magnificat—Mary's song itself—has been banned by those in power on three occasions in the last century: in India during British colonial rule; in Guatemala in the 1980s; and in Argentina after the Dirty War—out of fears that the Magnificat's apparently subversive message might incite revolution.

Mary indeed sings a song of revolution—a revolutionary hope that terrifies the powers that be—for she proclaims hope in an upside-down world—a radical and pervasive change—a canticle of the turning—a moment in history she will be a part of as she bears the impossible incarnation into the world—Emmanuel. And that Emmanuel—God with us—changes everything.

That Emmanuel—God with us—is the crux—the very hope we are to claim as people of God.

But sometimes hope is just hard. And yet as creative agents in God's creativity, we are called to bear God—to bear hope—even when we don't want to. We are called to bear God—bear hope— in situations that are not always easy, comfortable, or ideal. We are called to bear God—bear hope—so that great compassion and love overcome places of great sorrow, bigotry, closed-mindedness, and sadness. We are called to bear God even when we have great difficulty seeing the hope this incarnational revolution brings. But how?

Now, traditionally, scholars make the visit of Elizabeth and Mary centered around the men—you know, John and Jesus. They say we have this account in the Gospel to confirm the promises of God—to show how, when Mary arrived, John leapt inside Elizabeth's womb, recognizing the mother of God. They talk of the prophet cousins and how they—together—will change the world, and this meeting confirms that for the men. But I think there's more to the story than just the men (ever important as they are).

I think this story of Mary coming to Elizabeth is the Spirit understanding that Mary and Elizabeth need one another during this time.

Just think about it—after hearing she was to bear Emmanuel in the world, Mary is alone—suddenly, entirely, dangerously alone. No Gabriel beside her or Joseph or even her parents—only a gummy-bear-sized God inside her. And so Mary flees—toward her kin, toward refuge, toward sanctuary. And it is in the home of Elizabeth, in the company of her cousin, that Mary finds what she most needs. Elizabeth gathers and enfolds her. Welcomes her. Reminds her she is not alone.

Mary is not alone. Even in the midst of the ridiculous situation that was at hand—two women, one too old to bear a child, one so young she was not yet married, yet called to bear children of promise through whom God would change the world. And Mary and Elizabeth probably knew what little account the world would pay them, tucked away in the hill country, far from the courts of power and influence. And they probably knew how hard life was under the Roman Empire. Yet when faced with the long odds of their situation, they did not retreat or despair. They came together—weary as they may be, fiercely clinging on to one another—and out of that clinging, finding hope, for they were not alone.

And so they sang—Mary beginning, with Elizabeth joining in. They sang of their confidence in God's promise to upend the powers that be, reverse the fortunes of an unjust world, and lift up all those who had been oppressed. They sang not only of a God who will but of a God who already has begun this great redemption.

Mary sang, and then Elizabeth chimed in once she knew the words. They sang, and they sang, and they sang—together:

> My soul magnifies the Lord,
>   and my spirit rejoices in God my Savior,
>   for he has looked with favor on the lowliness of his servant.
>   Surely, from now on all generations will call me blessed;
>   for the Mighty One has done great things for me, and holy is his name.
> His mercy is for those who fear him
>   from generation to generation.
> He has shown strength with his arm;
>   he has scattered the proud in the thoughts of their hearts.
> He has brought down the powerful from their thrones,
>   and lifted up the lowly;
> he has filled the hungry with good things,
>   and sent the rich away empty.
> He has helped his servant Israel,

> in remembrance of his mercy,
> according to the promise he made to our ancestors,
> to Abraham and to his descendants forever.

Strangely, a song in a weary throat—sung. Wonderfully. Hope-filled. Together.

Together, Elizabeth and Mary reveal that the very thing we are invited into—hope—as we bear God in the world and sing of this upside down, topsy-turvy transformation, cannot be done without intimate connection with others. This Magnificat revolution cannot be sung without one another. We *need* each another. For when we hope, we hope not alone, but together. Like Elizabeth and Mary, when we plant our feet beside one another—creating space for each other, determined for God to answer when there seems to be silence—we do so together.

We support. We listen. We cry. Together.

We show up and stand with. We embrace vulnerability and courage. Together.

We hope on behalf of others when they can't utter the words. We sing the song when they cannot bring themselves to proclaim a melody. We do not bear God or bear hope in the world alone, but together.

Or, as Walter Brueggemann puts it, "Hope, on one hand, is an absurdity too embarrassing to speak about, for it flies in the face of all those claims we have been told are facts. Hope is the refusal to accept the reading of reality which is the majority opinion; and one does that only at great political and existential risk. On the other hand, hope is subversive, for it limits the grandiose pretension of the present, daring to announce that the present to which we have all made commitments is now called into question."[20]

Hope. Hope is still hard for me right now.

And maybe it's hard for you.

But when I think of how Mary did not have to hope alone, I'm comforted and think maybe, just maybe, the same is true for us. And I think maybe, just maybe, when we are together—when we recognize that we are not alone, when we understand we are called to be in intimate relationality with others—then that is when we can boldly sing the Magnificat revolution. That is when we can boldly enter into the inbreaking kingdom-turning of our world. That is when we can fiercely hope and dream and sing and act. That is when we can bear God in the world—together.

Even if all we have are just some weary throats joining in song—that was—and is—enough.

Thanks be to God.

This Week

Molly Brummett Wudel encourages us to join in singing, even if our throats are weary. Search through some music this week. What song is uplifting to you? Google or search YouTube for different arrangements of the Magnificat being sung. Search for "The Canticle of the Turning," and see what turns inside you.

Reflect on what a Magnificat revolution would look like. What powers would come tumbling down? Who would be lifted up? Who would be fed? How would God be proclaimed?

Questions for Reflection and Discussion

1. Molly Brummett Wudel says, "I don't know about you, but hope is hard for me these days. If I'm being completely honest, hope has been hard for me for a while now. Now I'm not talking about the temporary hope we have when we want this thing or that action to happen. I'm talking about the hope that comes with deep belief in the inbreaking kingdom of God—the rootedness in knowing God is at work in the world and in our own lives in such a way that it matters—that the way things are not the way things shall always be." What does this type of hope look like?

2. Molly also calls for a Magnificat revolution. What would that look like in this world? How might you participate in its inbreaking?

3. Maria Swearingen started her story by saying, "I came into the world one kind of Baptist and came out another kind." Her story of wrestling with her Baptist identity is common. If you are Baptist, why are you Baptist? If you follow another tradition, why have you found a home there?

4. Maria said, "Like Mary, we are carrying Jesus; we are carrying the Divine. We are carrying the hopes and dreams and visions that call us to love God and the world more fully." What are the wildest hopes and dreams you have for the world?

Endnotes

[1] Maria Swearingen, discussion with the author, October 13, 2016.

[2] Ibid.

[3] Ibid.

[4] Ibid.

[5] Ibid.

[6] Swearingen, "God, the Caroler," sermon preached at Daniel Chapel, Furman University, Greenville, South Carolina, December 6, 2015.

[7] Swearingen, discussion.

[8] Ibid.

[9] Molly Brummett Wudel, discussion with the author, October 12, 2016.

[10] Ibid.

[11] Steven Lipscomb, *Battle for the Minds*, directed by Steven Lipscomb (Louisville: PBS, 1997).

[12] Brummett Wudel, discussion.

[13] Ibid.

[14] Ibid.

[15] Brummett Wudel, "Mary: A Call to Revolution," sermon preached at Green Street United Methodist Church, Durham, North Carolina, July 15, 2012.

[16] Brummett Wudel, discussion.

WEEK FIVE
Promise

This study and these conversations delved into the deep waters of Baptist identity, the connection between sexuality, race, gender, and embodiment in space that was previously not a safe space and generational aspects of this call to preach.

Through conversations with women who were around at the very founding of the Alliance of Baptists to those who were born after its founding, the power of the organization became apparent. Key themes that continued to resurface—as if these preachers were sitting around a table in conversation with one another regarding their Baptist identities and preaching the Magnificat—were the importance of the freedom in being Baptist, embodiment as an act of gospel fulfillment, and the Magnificat as a call to agency, power, and revolution in their own lives and in the world.

Embodiment

Each preacher identified the times they are keenly aware that their bodies represent more than just their bodies when they step into the pulpit. Women across all denominations deal with comments about haircuts, dress, jewelry, shoes, and nail polish,[1] but these questions of identity and embodiment point to something far more incarnational that has been systematically excluded.

As churches were restructuring and stabilizing upon the creation of the Alliance of Baptists, there was still great resistance to women in pulpits. There is still resistance in many Baptist churches to women preaching or being pastors. Even when churches are welcoming, the statistics are not high even though enrollment at seminaries across the country is about equal.[2] Each of their stories of preaching began with what they had to overcome to get to the place where they even had the opportunity to preach and put their bodies in a pulpit.

Nancy Hastings Sehested reflected on the fact that often her body was the first female body to be in pulpits. It was startling for people to have a woman in the pulpit. As she preached and as congregants adjusted, they became more comfortable with a woman's a voice and body in a place—the pulpit, where it never before had been. Isabel Docampo was aware that her identity as a Cuban-American Baptist woman limited the places where she was welcome to preach and live into her call—ranging from seminary preaching classes to her position of working with refugees. April Baker was repeatedly told that she didn't belong because of her gender and sexuality. Kyndra Frazier recounted how her queer body was not welcome in the pulpits she grew up in and many where she continued to attend. Maria Swearingen told us that her queer, female self was viewed as the problem as she preached—in the same way Mary's pregnant body was viewed as the problem to be dealt with as she sang. And Molly Brummett Wudel knew that even thirty years after the formation of the Alliance of Baptists, her body was still not as welcome as others. These are the challenges these women face with the embodied work they do.

But the beauty of the full, embodied preaching they take part in overtakes the negative as they tell their stories. As Isabel Docampo said, "To stand in that pulpit, I am a witness to freedom and liberation. I stand there, showing that God breaks all these barriers. It shows the unconditional *hesed* of God."3

April Baker feels the tension and notes the power of her identity and when preaching: "Sometimes you do not even have to say a word. Your presence in the pulpit is the embodied you, and that preaches."4 Each preacher has examined what their presence in the pulpit means and claimed their embodiment as a gift from God, even while recognizing the culture might not welcome that embodied power.

Freedom in Being Baptist

Every preacher shared her struggle with wading through her Baptist identity. Some were born into the family, and some joined later in life and ministry. What each preacher identified, though, was the core commitment to Baptist freedoms. To be Baptist is to affirm each person's individual freedom in relationship with God. As Molly Brummett Wudel said, "Baptists are scrappy—and keenly in tune to freedom of the individual."[5]

This commitment to the freedom of being Baptist is fascinating given that the very aspect of committing to being Baptist also limits the ways in which each preacher could live out her call. They were systematically excluded from search committees, from pulpits, from positions, and even from reading Scripture during worship services because of their gender. When layered with sexuality, the options became even less and the discrimination even more. Yet this freedom is what each preacher returned to—as April Baker said, "Why not Baptist? We are a free church with opportunities and freedoms in our tradition."[6]

The freedoms of the Alliance covenant were especially named, appreciated, and held close by the preachers—both the ones who helped craft the statement and the ones who received it years later. The freedom of individual interpretation of the Bible, of the local church, of participation with the wider world, of servant leadership, of theological education, of work for justice, and of a free church in a free state still sound like good news to the six preachers and part of the reason they find a theological home within the Alliance of Baptists.

Agency, Power, Revolution

Commitment to Baptist freedoms and embodied preaching led these preachers to acknowledge how much the Magnificat pointed them back to their own agency and power as followers of God: "Being obedient to this call and those who have come before means we must preach. Baptist women must continue to claim space as pastors and preachers and not apologize for doing so."[7]

This agency, power, and revolution from Mary singing her Magnificat rang through all the preachers. Nancy Hastings Sehested said that in some of her most difficult and pain-filled moments, she would look to the generations before her—to the women preachers of the nineteenth century who were trying to do the same work as she with even less progress. They were still trying to get equal rights in civil society and in the church. Sehested would remind herself that the church was not going back this time, and that they would keep at it until this idea of women in ministry as as easy as breathing in and out." She looks to those women before her in the same way women younger than her reflect on her faithfulness and commitment to not go backward.

This power that comes from connecting Baptist identity to agency as understood through the Magnificat means that each person gets to sing—or preach—in their own way. The freedoms that these six preachers named demonstrates the space where co-creating with God, as Molly Brummett Wudel points out, can occur. Mary claimed her space in her singing even though it would not have been given to her by the larger culture at the time.

Mary's call to revolution was another aspect the preachers all pointed to as they worked through understanding themselves and the larger Baptist world. If they were going to have a revolution within Baptist life, it started with themselves. Nancy Hastings Sehested is aware that thirty years ago, the reason women weren't finding places to serve is because the church still held relative cultural power. Women would take whatever they could find in means of ministry positions—part-time, lousy-paying—just to find their way into a church. But this was a form of agency and power. By using the means they had, they pastored and preached, although these jobs were often called "ministering" and "teaching."

April Baker said it well when she shared that she would accept every invitation to speak in front of WMU or Girls in Action meetings because it meant that little girls would have a memory of a woman inhabiting a space usually reserved for a man. Little by little, the barriers were breaking down, and these women were changing what it looked like to be a pastor. The calls to justice in the Magnificat are viewed as the life's work of many of these preachers. It's a calling for these Baptist women preachers because their very identities depend on it. Their commitments and their understanding of the radical, welcoming love of God mean that justice is always there, always calling them to more action—to a revolution.

It is clear from these interviews and the themes drawn from the overlapping elements of the preachers' lives that the Magnificat has served as a formational text for each of them. Throughout their stories and their reflections, the Magnificat and Mary's story have guided these women preachers in ways of peace and justice and shepherded them in ways of accepting and celebrating their own identities.

If "to be Baptist means freedom," as Alan Neely said, then these six preachers are uniquely qualified to speak to both being Baptist and Baptist freedoms. Their sermons and their ministries embody the Baptist ideas of freedom of the individual and the local church as understood in the Alliance of Baptists' covenant. Their commitments to the priesthood of the believer offer a nuance on the wide-ranging, expansive calling of God on the lives of all people. They join in the giant chorus of voices singing the words of the Alliance covenant, which point to a song of liberation and love.

The Magnificat in the Gospel of Luke is a text where a woman is uniquely given the opportunity not just to speak, but to proclaim the good news. In this case, singing is an act of proclamation and protest. Mary sings of what she knows to be true of the faithfulness of God and what she believes is to come because of that faithfulness. The lives of these six preachers—Rev. Nancy Hastings Sehested, Rev. Dr. Isabel Docampo, Rev. April Baker, Rev. Kyndra Frazier, Rev. Maria Swearingen, and Rev. Molly Brummett Wudel—sing with the faithfulness of God and point us to the ever-loving, ever-creating power of God.

While holding all of these stories inside of me, I preached a sermon on the Magnificat in 2017 at Ravensworth Baptist Church, an Alliance of Baptists' congregational partner where I serve alongside Rev. Dr. Steve Hyde as pastor.

"Believe the Women"

A sermon preached by Rev. Dr. Leah Grundset Davis at Ravensworth Baptist Church, Annandale, Virginia, on December 17, 2017

Our third Sunday of Advent brings us to the Sunday of joy. I've loved looking at these songs in the Gospel of Luke and the way we have interacted with them. I don't know about you, but I've been listening to music differently these weeks—listening for the cries of hope, the verses of promise, and the songs of joy.

The Gospel of Luke has led us here to look at these songs, or canticles as they have traditionally been known. Luke's Gospel is unique from the others. In these first two chapters we've had angelic visitations, a priest struck mute in the temple, and Elizabeth and Mary pregnant miraculously. Luke frames his Gospel with faithful disciples from the very beginning to the very end. It's refreshing to read it that way—a new perspective perhaps—a twist on how we normally view the disciples, probably because in Luke's Gospel, these model disciples, these followers of Jesus…were all women.

Luke sandwiched his stories about Jesus teaching, preaching, his death and resurrection between Elizabeth and Mary singing ahead of time and Mary Magdalene, Joanna, Mary who found Jesus's tomb was empty and went to the disciples, singing a song of resurrection, only to told they were singing an idle tale with an idle tune. They sang these songs of joy and weren't listened to by the ones with power—not Joseph at first and not the disciples on the first Easter morning.

In Luke, Mary sings. Elizabeth blesses. The women at the tomb proclaim, and none of them are believed. I can almost hear Luke shouting to the church through the centuries, echoing a modern refrain of, "Believe the women. The women, too, have something to say about the state of the world and who Jesus is."

It's with that Advent framing of the Gospel of Luke that we look at our passage today where Mary sings her prophetic song of praise to God. We've jumped back in time from our encounter with Elizabeth and Zechariah the last two weeks. This passage today is before Elizabeth has given birth but after Zechariah is silenced.

The two women gather in the home of Zechariah, as it is called, both pregnant—Mary with Jesus, Elizabeth with John the Baptist. Mary had recently been visited by Gabriel, announcing her pregnancy, and Elizabeth was about six months along. When Elizabeth opened the door to her cousin Mary, she does so with joy. Here is Mary! Her beloved cousin. She blesses her, sings to her from right where she is—in the midst of her truth, right in the middle of her home, eighty years old, six months pregnant, with a husband who can't speak. Some might say that's not exactly the ideal situation to find yourself in, but Elizabeth doesn't sugarcoat her reality—she sings it. As Elizabeth sings, she does so in her context with her fear, her joy, her hope, her anxiety, her oppression, her privilege.

Elizabeth believes what Mary has told her, and look at verse 45. She says to Mary, "And blessed is she who believed that there would be a fulfillment of what was spoken to her by the Lord." Elizabeth believes Mary!

And calls her blessed. And then they keep singing. I imagine Elizabeth humming while Mary breaks out with what we now call the Magnificat.

A song burst out of Mary. A song of joy and praise. A song that placed her smack dab within her own world, her own context, and the joys and pains she knew so well. According to Nancy Hastings Sehested, she sang something like this:

> *I'm overflowing with thanks to God.*
> *I'm dancing to the song of God.*
> *God chose me, of all people.*
> *I'm blessed beyond words.*
> *God has done great things for me. Just look at me!*
> *God's mercy is endless.*
> *I hope my baby knows such mercy.*
> *I hope my baby knows a world full of God's creating,*
> *Where the high and mighty proud are put in their place—*
> *their place right alongside all of us.*
> *I hope my baby knows a world where tyrants and terrorists become harmless*
> *And those whose lives never mattered all matter.*
> *I hope my baby knows a world where the hungry have a taste of plenty*
> *And the overstuffed know the gnaw of hunger.*
> *I hope my baby knows a world where mercies pile higher than cruelties,*
> *And where the promise of peace cascades through every generation.*[8]

What a song to sing! Mary is overflowing with thanksgiving and dancing to the song of God. And as she sings within Zechariah's house, I wonder if she's looking around to see who is listening. Were Zechariah's priest-friends there? Was she worried that they might report her to the authorities with her topsy-turvy song of protest and resistance? Would her baby be safe? Would she be safe? Could she hardly contain herself because of the miracle that God-with-us was already within her?

Mary was singing in her truth, in all the ways she was created, all her fears and joys, and she sang of the justice-love of God and the promise of peace cascading through every generation. I believe her.

I mentioned that Nancy Hastings Sehested rewrote the Magnificat I just quoted. She is pastor at Circle of Mercy Congregation in Asheville, North Carolina, one of the founders of the Alliance of Baptists, and one of the first women to be a pastor back when there were no women pastors, decades ago. She went through a lot in those years—painful exclusions, threats, and no place to hang her pulpit robe. When I spoke with her last year about this very passage, she told me that she's preached on this passage more than anything else because it comes around each year in the lectionary. She said Mary's song gave her strength to stand in her truth, sing her song to the powers that be—which happened to be the Baptist powers of the day.

I love the way Nancy interpreted Mary's song with the piece about "where the high and mighty proud are put in their place—their place right alongside all of us." Whew. That gets at it, doesn't it? This song of Mary is the lifting up of the lowly and the knocking down of the powerful, but what that means is that this song points us to the justice-love of God—where we are all equal. The high and mighty proud are put in their place—right alongside everybody.

"I hope my baby knows those who lives who never mattered to the world—they matter." Mary sings that, and I think it's safe to say her son, Jesus, got the concept of the lives of the most oppressed, most occupied, as being the ones that need attention.

I don't know this, but as Nancy rewrote that, I imagine this was a way for her to sing her truth and, even in the midst of all of it, keep singing of the radical justice-love of God. I believe Nancy.

When we situate ourselves in our truth and proclaim from that place, it is powerful. You all may remember when the missions commission hosted the annual Fall Ethics Seminar, they welcomed Rev. Dr. Sharon Stanley-Rea from the Disciples of Christ, who is the director of immigrant and refugee ministries. As she was talking to us about the many issues facing our country and, specifically, the marginalized people who are immigrants and refugees, she specifically spoke of the Dreamers and how young people are afraid to tell their stories, afraid to emerge from the shadows for fear that they will be deported.

She told one story about a young woman, Maria, who is a Dreamer from Fresno, California. Her context had been unfriendly, and she had been understandably hesitant to share her story publicly in the area. There was a big Dream Act rally being held outside the White House a few months ago, and Maria was here. She was talking with Sharon the night before the rally of her fears and anxieties. The next morning, she got to the rally, and something compelled her to stand up. Remember, this was in front of the White House of the United States, with the administration inside that was threatening her safety, her status, and her future.

And you know what Maria did? She got right up on the stage, and she told her story. She told of her arrival in the United States, the way she excelled in school, her devoted family, and the hopes she had for the future. She sang in that space her truth of who she was and the context of her day. Sharon said there were no dry eyes because of the power with which Maria communicated, the song that came to her lips of the hope and promise she dreamed of. A song of justice-love. I believe Maria.

The Rev. T. Denise Anderson, co-moderator of the Presbyterian Church (USA), writes, "We generally don't believe women because what they have to say hurts us. If they told the truth—as many currently are—our notions of the inherent goodness of people would be irreparably shattered. When women speak, humanity is exposed."9 When women speak, humanity is exposed.

Mary's song compels us to sing our own. How would you rewrite the song of finding yourself in the place where life is uncertain, you are scared, and yet there's a bit of hope on the horizon, something is brimming with new life? What song of God is about to burst forth from your lips—is it a cry of lament? A joy-filled chorus? Is it a song that ushers in a new way of being for all of us? Do you have some Advent-joy that you're trying to stuff down inside of you but some notes keep squeaking out of your mouth?

What might the world sound like if we all sang our songs about God's justice-love as boldly as Mary did? Our songs would be powerful and point us to new understandings of God and one another. We would believe each other!

When we can't sing, during those hard times when the words can't even form, I fall back on Mary's song as a place to begin and reorient myself. Because I believe her.

I believe her that God is making all things new. I believe her that God looked on her and all that represented, and she said yes to birthing the ultimate love into the world.

I believe her that God's mercy is for the Dreamers and everyone else, that the proud will be scattered and the powerful knocked down from their thrones or oval offices or halls of Congress or Hollywood studios.

I believe her that God has lifted up the lowly to empower them and amplify their songs that the world needs to hear so we can all more fully be ourselves.

I believe that God's radical love came in the form of Jesus to live among us, that we might fully understand ourselves, each other, and God.

I believe Mary. I believe the women at the tomb who said, "Christ is risen!" I believe Nancy and Maria. I believe you and your songs and stories. We have these songs of joy and hope and resurrection.

Let's be bold and sing our songs, whether we sing offkey or with the most tuned soprano voice. Sing boldly and believe! God is with us.

Thanks be to God. Amen.

This Week

Reflect on all that you have studied and sat with over these last few weeks. On a piece of paper, write out of the Magnificat, line by line. Which line is the most comforting? Which one is the most disturbing? Color it, mark it up, hold the space sacred as you engage with the text.

Questions for Reflection and Discussion

1. In Leah's sermon she says, "I believe the women." As women's voices are given more of an audience, what do you believe about what they are saying?

2. What stories are you hearing in church? on social media? in the news?

What conclusions did you draw about the stories and sermons that were shared?

3. Can you think of anyone who has broken through a barrier (pulpit or otherwise) to live into the fullness of who God created them to be?

4. What has been your journey through this study? What have you learned about yourself?

Endnotes

[1] Amy McCullough, "Her Preaching Body: A Qualitative Study of Agency, Meaning and Proclamation in Contemporary Female Preachers" (PhD diss., Vanderbilt University, 2012), 127–137.

[2] Pam Durso and Kevin Pranato, "Baptist Women in Ministry: State of Women in Baptist Life Report 2015" (paper presented at the annual meeting of Baptist Women in Ministry, Winston-Salem, June 26, 2016), 3.

[3] Isabel Docampo, discussion with the author, October 26, 2016.

[4] April Baker, discussion with the author, October 19, 2016.

[5] Molly Brummett Wudel, discussion with the author, October 12, 2016.

[6] Baker, discussion.

[7] Brummett Wudel, discussion.

[8] Nancy Hastings Sehested, "All's Wild with the World: A Sermon on Mary's Magnificat," sermon preached at Circle of Mercy Congregation, December 7, 2016.

[9] T. Denise Anderson as quoted by Stephanie Sorge Wing, "I Believe the Women," The Young Clergy Women Project, December 5, 2017.

Leader's Guide/Lesson Plan

Following is a suggested outline for a five-week study (approximately one hour per session). Depending on your group and their comfort with one another, time may be extended for the opening question, or you might dive right into the discussion. Invite different people to participate in the prayer times and the reading of the Luke text each week.

Week One: Hope

During the Week

Email the group with a question to consider, including one quote from the section that you'd like to discuss further, or use the following example:

Leah Grundset Davis wrote, "We sing Mary's song with joy because now it is ours to sing—we are all the mothers of God, birthing God's love into a world desperate for it." When is a time that a song changed you? Can you think of a song that has moved you?

Gather (5 minutes)

As you gather, mark the beginning of your discussion time together by lighting a candle and reading the Magnificat. Invite someone to offer an opening centering prayer.

Opening Question (10 minutes)

Based on the email from the week before, share a song that has moved you. What is the song? How does it make you feel? Describe the context surrounding the time you heard this song.

Walk through the Questions for Discussion and Reflection
(20–30 minutes)

1. How do you think Mary felt when she approached Elizabeth's home?

2. How does Mary's song speak to our world today? How does she point to God's activity in the world?

3. Does this passage from Mary sound like good news to you? Does it seem like an expression of God's abundance in the world?

4. What do you think it meant for Jesus to grow up with a mother like Mary? Do you think he heard this song again in his young life?

5. Have there been songs in your life that influenced you and formed you in faith? Hymns at church? A song your family sang together growing up? A song or chant or protest song that brought you hope? Listen to that song and see what emerges within you. Do you feel centered? Inspired?

6. Invite participants to share what song they wrote or illustrated this week. How did the experience of the Magnificat sit with them?

Closing (5 minutes)

Invite any closing thoughts.

End with a benediction:

"The surprises of God's spirit are still bringing new life amid the miracle and mess of it all, and we are bodying forth the good news of God's transforming love."

—Nancy Hastings Sehested

Week Two: Peace

During the Week

Email the group with a question to consider, including one quote from the section that you'd like to discuss further, or use the following example:

"Nancy Hastings Sehested has always felt a connection with Mary and the Magnificat and has preached many sermons in her career on the Lukan passage. She has likened the context of Mary's song to herself, the church, and the Alliance of Baptists. Throughout her career she witnessed various power dynamics in the church and in society. People sometimes think of Mary as powerless, Sehested said. She lived in a violent and hostile world, and yet she courageously lived her call with all that was within her." How does this quote about Nancy Hastings Sehested settle with you? Does her identification with Mary make sense to you? Have you ever identified with Mary, or can you think of someone who has?

Gather (5 minutes)

As you gather, mark the beginning of your discussion time together by lighting a candle and reading the Magnificat. Invite someone to offer an opening centering prayer.

Opening Question (10 minutes)

Based on the email from the week before, ask how Nancy Hastings Sehested's identification with Mary singing the Magnificat settled with them. Have they ever identified with Mary? How did they hear Mary's song differently as embodied in Nancy's life?

Walk through the Questions for Discussion and Reflection
(20–30 minutes)

1. What unique challenges did Nancy Hastings Sehested and Isabel Docampo face in their callings?

2. Nancy said that Mary "calls her back to herself." What do you think about that? Do you identify with her statement about Mary?

3. Isabel shares her story about taking a trip to Cuba and being invited to preach and experiencing the intersection of her identities. Have you

ever had a moment like that? Has anyone encouraged you to take a full look at all the identities you carry?

4. How does the Magnificat sound coming from these two different preachers? With whom do you identify?

5. At the end of Isabel's sermon, she asks the congregation, "Will you join God in bearing witness? Will you sing?" To what are you being called to bear witness? What song are you being called to sing?

6. If you also claim Baptist identity, how do these stories help you understand what being Baptist means to you?

Closing (5 minutes)

Invite any closing thoughts.

End with a benediction:

"Our souls magnify the Lord.... God has regard for the humble state of these, God's servants. We are endowed with all that God needs. Nothing can take that away from us, and so we exalt our God."

—Isabel Docampo

Week Three: *Joy*

During the Week

Email the group with a question to consider, including one quote from the section that you'd like to discuss further, or use the following example:

For Kyndra Frazier to accept her full identity and stand behind a pulpit is powerful for her. It's a gift to her and to the world to fully embrace her identity: "It's still audacious to be in someone's pulpit when people believe that you aren't supposed to be preaching. But God transcends respectability politics, legalism, and religious dogma. We can't allow people to get in the way of what God has called us to do and be in the world. That's where Mary was. It's powerful to see her transformation."

What would it look like for you to accept your full identity? How does Kyndra's story and her connection with Mary accepting her full identity speak to you?

Gather (5 minutes)

As you gather, mark the beginning of your discussion time together by lighting a candle and reading the Magnificat. Invite someone to offer an opening centering prayer.

Opening Question (10 minutes)

Based on the email from the week before, ask the group what would it look like for you to accept your full identity? How does Kyndra's story and her connection with Mary accepting her full identity speak to you?

Walk through the Questions for Discussion and Reflection (20–30 minutes)

1. April Baker said, "The Magnificat speaks most clearly to me about the powerful voice of someone who is not allowed to have a voice." When is a time you felt like you didn't have a voice? Did you linger in that space? Speak up anyway? How does Mary's voice strengthen your own?

2. Kyndra Frazier spends time talking about the strength of the women who went before her in her family and in her church growing up. These women passed down a legacy to her. Who in your life has pointed

you toward God and shared a legacy with you? To whom are you passing something down?

3. In April's sermon she mentions two girls in her congregation who care for one another, modeling the relationship between Mary and Elizabeth. What cherished friendships do you have in your life? How do they point you toward God?

4. Kyndra tells us about her connection to Mary's Magnificat in the way it empowered her to claim her full self as a revealing of God's creative power. What part of you do you need to dust off and spend some time with?

Closing (5 minutes)
Invite any closing thoughts.

End with a benediction:
"Mary said yes to God and to herself. It's a different thing when we say God accepts us but we don't accept ourselves. Mary gave herself a yes, and it's a celebration! So say YES to yourselves! Love yourselves!"

—Kyndra Frazier

"Use your voice and sing the song that's in your heart. When you've encountered the holy, there is something of yours to bear in the world. So do it. Do it through art, preaching, kindness, presence. Sing it!"

—April Baker

Week Four: Love

During the Week

Email the group with a question to consider, including one quote from the section that you'd like to discuss further, or use the following example:

In Maria Swearingen's sermon "Great with Child" she said, "I suppose, though, that we could gaze upon Mary, great with child, and leave ourselves outside of the picture. I suppose we could hold this moment at arm's length and consider its abstract meaning without entering inside of it more deeply. But the stories in Scripture are not meant for analysis or detachment. They are meant to captivate our imaginations and revive our visions. So maybe this evening we can place ourselves in Mary's shoes or sandals or even bare feet. Maybe for a few moments while we are gathered here, we can imagine our own pregnancies…perhaps for some of us that's literal. But for many of us, we may need to press beyond the literal and imagine our souls as a womb…giving life and energy and love to whatever is growing inside of us."

What does it look like for us to put ourselves in the picture, birthing something new into the world? How are our visions revived?

Gather (5 minutes)

As you gather, mark the beginning of your discussion time together by lighting a candle and reading the Magnificat. Invite someone to offer an opening centering prayer.

Opening Question (10 minutes)

Based on the email from the week before, ask the group about what Maria Swearingen said in her sermon about putting ourselves in the picture alongside Mary. What does it look like for us to put ourselves in the picture, birthing something new into the world? How are our visions revived?

Walk through the Questions for Discussion and Reflection
(20–30 minutes)

1. Molly Brummett Wudel says, "I don't know about you, but hope is hard for me these days. If I'm being completely honest, hope has been hard for me for a while now. Now, I'm not talking about the

temporary 'hope' we have when we want this thing or that action to happen. I'm talking about the hope that comes with deep belief in the inbreaking kingdom of God—the rootedness in knowing God is at work in the world and in our own lives in such a way that it matters—that the way things are is not the way things shall be." What does this type of hope look like?

2. Molly also calls for a Magnificat revolution. What would that look like in this world? How might you participate in its inbreaking?

3. Maria Swearingen starts her story by saying, "I came into the world one kind of Baptist and came out another kind." Her story of wrestling with her Baptist identity is common. If you are Baptist, why are you Baptist? If you follow another tradition, why have you found a home there?

4. Maria said, "Like Mary, we are carrying Jesus; we are carrying the Divine. We are carrying the hopes and dreams and visions that call us to love God and the world more fully." What are the wildest hopes and dreams you have for the world?

Closing (5 minutes)
Invite any closing thoughts.

End with a benediction:
"We would willingly and boldly embrace the revolution of the Magnificat and dance in that truth in our whole beings, in the world, and in our churches. We would embody the Magnificat in all we do."
—Molly Brummett Wudel

"Disruption comes when you claim embodiment. As people problematize who you are based on your presence, keep singing. There is an ancient song that keeps showing up, and you get to claim it."
—Maria Swearingen

Week Five: Promise

During the Week

Email the group with a question to consider, or use the following example:

What has been your journey through this study? What have you learned about yourself?

Gather (5 minutes)

As you gather, mark the beginning of your discussion time together by lighting of a candle and reading the Magnificat. Invite someone to offer an opening centering prayer.

Opening Question (10 minutes)

Based on the email from the week before, ask, "What has been your journey through this study? What have you learned about yourself?"

Walk through the Questions for Discussion and Reflection (20–30 minutes)

In Leah Grundset Davis's sermon, she says, "I believe the women." As women's voices are given more of an audience, what do you believe about what they are saying?

What stories are you hearing in church? on social media? in the news?

What conclusions did you draw about the stories and sermons that were shared?

Can you think of anyone who has broken through a barrier (pulpit or otherwise) to live into the fullness of God created them to be?

Closing (5 minutes)

Invite any closing thoughts.

End with a benediction:

"Hope, peace, joy, and love have put on flesh and moved into the neighborhood! Go into this night of wonder fully human, fully giving thanks to God."

—Leah Grundset Davis

Sermon Series and Worship Services for the Seasons of Advent and Christmas

The Gospel of Luke offers a number of songs or canticles in the early chapters that are a way to navigate and experience the seasons of Advent and Christmas. Singing is such an important and beloved part of our time of preparation and celebration of the birth of Jesus, so pairing texts about songs alongside our sacred hymns provides depth with our church year and scripture.

Advent 1: Sing a Song of Hope

Zechariah's song about Jesus ushers us into the season of Advent. Zechariah's song has two parts. The first is his song about Jesus. Next week, we'll look at his song about his own son, John the Baptist. What might it mean that from his silence, Zechariah breaks forth in song? What is Luke showing us about proclamation and singing?

Texts for the Day
Malachi 3:1–4   Philippians 1:3-11
*Luke 1:57–75

Call to Worship
Advent people, we proclaim, "Blessed be the Lord!"
for God has looked favorably on his people and redeemed them.
The Lord has raised up a mighty savior for us
in the house of his servant David, as he spoke through the mouth of his holy prophets from of old,
that we would be saved from our enemies.
We sing a song of God's hope—from all generations until now.
We light this candle of hope to remind us that God is with us, even as we wait.
Let us worship God!

Children's Sermon
Each week, you'll be creating a picture, both literally and metaphorically, of hope, peace, joy, love, promise, and celebration. Find a large newsprint or poster (you could even do a different poster for each week). Divide it into six sections (hope, peace, joy, love, promise, and celebration). Consider writing the weeks of Advent in purple and Christmas Eve and the first Sunday of Christmas in yellow or gold to follow liturgical traditions.

For Advent 1, take your poster with the word *hope*, and invite the children to share what hope means to them. What do they hope for? Give each child a sticker, and invite them to place the sticker on the poster board surrounding the word hope to represent their hopes for their world, themselves, their church.

Prayer: God, help me sing a song of hope to all I meet. Amen.

Suggested Hymns
O Come, O Come, Emmanuel
O, How a Rose Ere Blooming
Come, O Long Expected Jesus
Blessed Be the God of Israel

Benediction
"Use your voice, and sing the song that's in your heart. When you've encountered the holy, there is something of yours to bear in the world. So do it. Do it through art, preaching, kindness, presence. Sing it!"

—April Baker

Advent 2: Sing a Song of Peace

Zechariah's song about John the Baptist welcomes a song of peace. What does Zechariah, a priest in the temple, sing about his son? What does he hope for him and for the world? What do you think Elizabeth is thinking as he sings this song? Where is Elizabeth during this song?

Texts for the Day
Isaiah 40:1–5   Colossians 1:11–20
*Luke 1:76–80

Call to Worship
Advent people, we proclaim, "Blessed be the Lord!"
for God has looked favorably on his people and redeemed them.
The Lord has raised up a mighty savior for us
in the house of his servant David, as he spoke through the mouth of his holy prophets from of old,
that we would be saved from our enemies.
We sing a song of God's peace—from all generations until now.
We light this candle of peace to remind us that God is with us, even as we wait.
Let us worship God!

Children's Sermon

For Advent 2 return to the second part of your poster and the word *peace*. Print off pictures of doves or olive branches. Give these to the children, and explain what these traditional symbols mean. As they return to their seats or their classes, invite them to color the sheets and consider how they can bring peace into the world. Place one of these printouts on the section marked *peace* on your poster.

Prayer: God, you showed us how to hope last week. Help us to bring peace to our world, our families, and ourselves. Amen.

Suggested Hymns
O Come, O Come, Emmanuel
Prepare the Way of the Lord!
Let All Mortal Flesh Keep Silence
Blessed Be the God of Israel

Benediction
"Disruption comes when you claim embodiment. As people problematize who you are based on your presence, keep singing. There is an ancient song that keeps showing up, and you get to claim it."
—Maria Swearingen

Advent 3: Sing a Song of Joy

Mary's song on the traditional Advent Sunday of joy brings about a joy that goes beyond happiness. Mary's song is of the fullness of God's dream for the world—one where equity and love reign. Consider inviting a woman to proclaim on Advent 3 when the Magnificat is the text. What would it mean for your congregation to hear a woman preach the words of Mary if they normally hear from a man? What might it mean for children in the congregation to hear the embodied words of Mary from a woman?

Texts for the Day
Isaiah 61:1–4, 8–11   1 Thessalonians 5:16–24
*Luke 1:39–56

Call to Worship
Advent people, we proclaim, "Our souls magnify the Lord!"
Our spirits rejoice in God, our savior, and holy is God's name!
God elevates the lowly, releases the captive, fills the hungry with good things, brings sight to the blind.
We rejoice in God's justice-love, which is faithful to all generations.
We light this candle of joy to remind us that God is with us, even as we wait.
Let us worship God!

Children's Sermon
For your third section of your poster, focus on joy. Invite the children to spell *joy* loudly during the children's time, and invite the congregation to chant *J-O-Y* with you. The kids will love feeling like it's rowdy when they are leading the adults. Consider depicting joy on your poster with bright, large letters. Invite the children to share a time when they felt joy. Read the Magnificat to them from *The Message*, and share about how Mary felt joy.

Prayer: God, we learned about hope and peace and now joy during this season of Advent. Help us see joy around us. Amen.

Suggested Hymns
Joy to the World
There's a Song in the Air
Joyful, Joyful, We Adore Thee

Benedictions
"Mary said yes to God and to herself. It's a different thing when we say God accepts us but we don't accept ourselves. Mary gave herself a yes, and it's a celebration! So say YES to yourselves! Love yourselves!"
—Kyndra Frazier

"We would willingly and boldly embrace the revolution of the Magnificat and dance in that truth in our whole beings, in the world, and in our churches. We would embody the Magnificat in all we do."
—Molly Brummett Wudel

Darkest Night Service: Sing a Song of Grief

Many churches offer a longest night service or service of consolation during the Advent season. The holidays stir up grief and trauma that many of us have experienced. Consider including this service thematically within your Advent and Christmas series so that it is part of how your church worships and not an extra service on the side. Continue with the words and songs of Scripture that offer space for grief and joy to exist side by side. Mary's song is powerful and engages the reality of grief and pain alongside the hoped-for world of God.

*Luke 1:39–56

Call to Worship
Our God is with us here today.
In our sadness, our grief, our loss, the God of hope sits alongside us.
We see kindness in the face of strangers and know that God is with us.
Let us worship God.

Suggested Hymns
Come, O Long Expected Jesus
O Come, O Come, Emmanuel
Instrumental, reflective music

Benediction
"Go into this night knowing that you are God's beloved and that your song of grief is received, held, and honored. You are loved. Go in peace."
—Leah Grundset Davis

Advent 4: Sing a Song of Love

Many churches will read the traditional Christmas story this Sunday and again on Christmas Eve. Examine them differently each time. On this fourth and final Sunday of Advent, look at the songs of the angels and shepherds as the least likely voices to proclaim what is happening in the world. Who would have ever thought they would be the ones to make the announcement?

Texts for the Day
Luke 2:1–20   Isaiah 9:2–7

Call to Worship
Advent people, we have been watching and waiting and singing!
The people who walked in darkness have seen a great light.
Those who lived in a land of darkness—on them, light has shined.
We sing, "Glory to God in the highest heaven!"
We light this candle of love to remind us that God is with us.
Let us worship God!

Children's Sermon
For the fourth Sunday of Advent, it's all about love. Order some temporary tattoos for the children that say *love* on them. Pass those out, and give them a few extra to share with others. As we look at the fourth section of our poster, adhere some of those tattoos surrounding the larger word *love*. Reflect on the Advent journey so far—hope, peace, joy, and love. What have they learned about God and the ways they wait for Jesus to be born?

Prayer: God, you love us, and we love you. May we all love each other. Amen.

Suggested Hymns
Angels We Have Heard on High
O Come, All Ye Faithful
Hark! The Herald Angels Sing
Angels from the Realms of Glory

Benediction

"The surprises of God's spirit are still bringing new life amid the miracle and mess of it all, and we are bodying forth the good news of God's transforming love."

—Nancy Hastings Sehested

Christmas Eve: Sing a Song of Promise

Jesus has been born! Sing the song of promise that extends to all of creation of wholeness, hope, peace, joy, and love. The good news is among us!

Text for the Day
Luke 2:1–20

Call to Worship
Advent people, we have been watching and waiting and singing!
The people who walked in darkness have seen a great light.
Those who lived in a land of darkness—on them, light has shined.
We sing, "Glory to God in the highest heaven!"
Tonight, we light the Christ candle, for today in the city of David, a Savior has been born; he is Christ the Lord!
Let us worship God!

Children's Sermon
Hold up your nearly completed poster. How exciting to see it being decorated to fullness on this special night. As you read the passage from Luke to the children, ask them to listen for moments of hope, peace, joy, and love. Share of God's promises with the world and God's promise to always love them. Share what Jesus's birth means to you in how you understand God's love.

Prayer: God, thank you for Jesus's birth and all the ways he taught us to live and sing. Amen.

Suggested Hymns
O Come, All Ye Faithful
Silent Night
O Little Town of Bethlehem
Joy to the World
Angels We Have Heard on High
Away in a Manger

Benediction

"Hope, peace, joy, and love have put on flesh and moved into the neighborhood! Go into this night of wonder fully human, fully giving thanks to God."

—Leah Grundset Davis

Christmas 1: Sing a Song of Celebration

Simeon's song in the second chapter of Luke sings of fulfillment and longing like no other passage about the birth of Jesus. What does Simeon's song of praise speak to us? How do you think Anna felt?

Texts for the Day
Luke 2:22–40   Galatians 4:4–7
Isaiah 61:10–62:3

Call to Worship
Christmas people, Emmanuel, God-with-us, has come!
We sing because our eyes have seen God's salvation!
We sing because the light is shining in the world!
We sing a song of celebration because Jesus reveals peace, hope, joy, and love to all.
Let us worship God!

Children's Sermon
Holding up your fully decorated poster, invite the children to process in at the beginning of worship. As they gather for the children's time, invite them to share what they have learned, and have them lead the congregation in one of your favorite hymns as a time of celebration.

Prayer: Sung benediction of your congregation's favorite hymn.

Suggested Hymns
Go, Tell It on the Mountain!
Joy to the World

Benediction
"Our souls magnify the Lord.... God has regard for the humble state of these, God's servants. We are endowed with all that God needs. Nothing can take that away from us, and so we exalt our God."

—Isabel Docampo

Ideas for Worship Engagement

Singing Our Songs: Invite congregation members to share their songs—their stories that tell of hope, peace, joy, and love. How might you incorporate these powerful songs of present day into your worship series?

Worship Leadership: Some members might have worked through this study. They might have written a poem or a prayer. If there is a group within your congregation working through this study, consider having them participate in worship each week—lighting the Advent candle, offering the prayers, leading or writing the calls to worship, offering testimony, and reading Scripture. They will have embodied these texts after living with them.

For More Information

Resources

Alliance of Baptists. "Covenant & Mission." Alliance of Baptists. Last modified April 2013. Accessed November 2, 2016. http://allianceofbaptists.org/OurAlliance/covenant_and_mission.

Anders, Sarah Francis. "Tracing Past and Present." In *The New Has Come*. Edited by Anne Thomas Neil. Washington: Southern Baptist Alliance, 1989.

Bailey, Judith Bledsoe. *Strength for the Journey: Feminist Theology and Baptist Women Pastors*. Richmond: Center for Baptist Heritage and Studies, 2015.

Baker, April. "The Mystery You Behold." Sermon, Glendale Baptist Church, Nashville, December 20, 2015.

Campbell-Reed, Eileen. *Anatomy of a Schism: How Clergywomen's Narratives Reinterpret the Fracturing of the Southern Baptist Convention*. Knoxville: University of Tennessee Press, 2016.

Dault, Jennifer Harris, ed. *The Modern Magnificat: Women Responding to the Call of God*. Macon: Nurturing Faith, 2014.

Durber, Susan. *Preaching Like a Woman*. London: Society for Promoting Christian Knowledge, 2007.

Durso, Pam and Johns, LeeAnn Gunter, eds. *The World Is Waiting for You: Celebrating the 50th Anniversary of the Ordination of Addie Davis*. Macon: Smyth & Helwys Publishing, 2014.

Durso, Pam and Pranato, Kevin. "Baptist Women in Ministry: State of Women in Baptist Life Report 2015." Paper presented at the annual meeting of Baptist Women in Ministry, Winston-Salem, June 26, 2016.

Flowers, Elizabeth H. *Into the Pulpit*. Chapel Hill: University of North Carolina Press, 2014.

Gardner, Andrew. *Reimagining Zion: A History of the Alliance of Baptists*. Macon: Nurturing Faith, 2015.

Leonard, Bill J. *Baptist Ways: A History*. Valley Forge: Judson Press, 2003.

Levine, Amy-Jill, ed. *A Feminist Companion to Luke*. London: Sheffield Academic Press, 2002.

Lipscomb, Steven. *Battle for the Minds*. Directed by Steven Lipscomb. Lousiville: PBS, 1997.

McBeth, Leon. "Baptist Beginnings." The Baptist History and Heritage Society Blog, 1979. Accessed November 12, 2016. http://www.baptisthistory.org/baptistorigins/baptistbeginnings.html.

McCullough, Amy. "Her Preaching Body: A Qualitative Study of Agency, Meaning and Proclamation in Contemporary Female Preachers." PhD diss., Vanderbilt University, 2012.

Menhinick, Keith. "My Kind of People." Alliance of Baptists, April 27, 2015. Accessed January 6, 2017. http://allianceofbaptists.org/PCP/alliance_blog_detail/aobgathering-my-kind-of-people-by-keith-a.-menhinick.

Neely, Alan. *Being Baptist Means Freedom*. Charlotte: Southern Baptist Alliance, 1988.

Newsome, Carol A., Ringe, Sharon H., and Lapsley, Jacqueline E., eds. *Women's Bible Commentary*. Louisville: Westminster John Knox Press, 2012.

Ringe, Sharon H. *Luke*. Louisville: Westminster John Knox Press, 1995.

Rivera, Mayra. *The Touch of Transcendence: A Postcolonial Theology of God*. Louisville: Westminster John Knox Press, 2007.

Ruether, Rosemary Radford. *Mary: The Feminine Face of the Church*. Philadelphia: Westminster Press, 1977.

Sehested, Nancy Hastings. "Hopes and Fears." Sermon, Circle of Mercy Congregation, Asheville, December 21, 2014.

Swearingen, Maria. "God, the Caroler." Sermon, Daniel Chapel, Furman University, Greenville, December 6, 2015.

Wudel, Molly Brummett. "Mary: A Call to Revolution." Sermon, Green Street United Methodist Church, Durham, July 15, 2012.

Interviews

Baker, April. Interview by Leah Grundset Davis. Personal interview. Virtual interview. October 19, 2016.

Dempsey, Paula Clayton. Interview by Leah Grundset Davis. Personal interview. In person interview, Silver Spring, Maryland. November 1, 2014.

Docampo, Isabel. Interview by Leah Grundset Davis. Personal interview. Virtual interview. October 26, 2016.

Frazier, Kyndra. Interview by Leah Grundset Davis. Personal interview. Virtual interview. Ocober 31, 2016.

Sehested, Nancy Hastings. Interview by Leah Grundset Davis. Personal interview. Virtual interview. October 26, 2016.

Swearingen, Maria. Interview by Leah Grundset Davis. Personal interview. Virtual interview. October 13, 2016.

Wudel, Molly Brummett. Interview by Leah Grundset Davis. Personal interview. Virtual interview. October 12, 2016

www.ingramcontent.com/pod-product-compliance
Lightning Source LLC
Chambersburg PA
CBHW071006160426
43193CB00012B/1937